# I choose to be wealthy.
# I choose to be successful.
# Financial independence
# is mine.
# I now see myself as a prosperous person.
# Large amounts of money are coming to me.

☞          ☜

For some people, just repeating these affirmations with feeling many times daily is all it takes to bring them financial wealth. You may become one of those people, and Robert Griswold can help you get there. He has developed an entire program that puts you in charge of your destiny and empowers you to make the kind of money you've dreamed about, enjoy high self-esteem, and live a happier, more fulfilled life. His own career success and that of thousands of others who have attended his workshops and listened to his audio tapes are proof of the tremendous potential that lies within each one of us. You can start using this program right now—and start learning...

# HOW TO ATTRACT MONEY

ROBERT GRISWOLD is founder and President of Effective Learning Systems, Inc., whose Board of Advisors includes Bernie Siegel, Raymond Moody, C. Norman Shealy, and O. Carl Simonton. The former president of three corporations, Robert Griswold has combined the most current brain/mind research, sound psychological principles, effective mind development techniques, and years of experience working with thousands of people to produce his acclaimed programs in areas such as peak performance in sports, personal magnetism, self-confidence, weight loss, immunity and longevity, and business success.

# HOW TO ATTRACT MONEY

## Robert Griswold

**WARNER BOOKS**

A Time Warner Company

Warner Books, Inc., 1271 Avenue of the Americas, New York, NY 10020

Ⓦ A Time Warner Company

Printed in the United States of America

First printing: January 1993

10 9 8 7 6 5 4 3 2 1

Library of Congress Cataloging-in-Publication Data
Griswold, Robert E.
    How to attract money / Robert E. Griswold.
        p.    cm.
    ISBN 0-446-39331-2
        1. Finance, Personal—Psychological aspects.    2. Money—Psychological aspects.    3. Schemas (Psychology)    4. Self-realization.    I. Title.
    HG179.G747    1993
    332.024—dc20
                                                    92-1220
                                                    CIP

Book design by H. Roberts
Cover design by Mike Stromberg

I dedicate this book to my father,
William Dunn Griswold.
He never had much money, but was rich in
every other way.
I'll always love him.

# ACKNOWLEDGMENTS

You will soon see that this book is not just about money. It's about living successfully and enjoying abundance in the process. Therefore I feel compelled to acknowledge at least some of the people who have helped me to live as successfully as I have, and consequently have helped me write this book.

I'll start with my Mom and Dad, who did their best to raise their four sons to be independent and responsible. And they were always there when I needed them. Then come my three brothers: Bill, who taught me generosity at an early age; Bud, who taught me to be a "go-getter"; and Jim, ten years my junior, who looked up to me and caused me to at least try to be a good example, and in recent years has been a valuable coworker.

My wife Deirdre deserves tons of credit for believing in me before I believed in myself, and providing a great deal of inspiration and assistance in business.

In the past twenty years I have been very fortunate to have worked with and learned from some of the greatest people in the fields of psychology, medicine, education, and the broad area of human potential development.

One of these people was Buckminster Fuller who was a great teacher as well as an architect, engineer, poet, inventor, author, futurist, mathematician, etc., etc., etc. He taught me that if I just do my best to make a positive contribution to the planet and its inhabitants, whatever money I need will be forthcoming.

Richard and Leslie Bach deserve thanks for insisting that I "hang in there" when I became discouraged in my early attempts to write a book.

José Silva taught me, and millions of others, about the potential of the mind, and some effective ways of tapping that potential.

I once told Norman Cousins that although I had no heroes since childhood, he was a hero to me. He was a courageous, intelligent, warm, friendly man whose advice and support meant a lot to me. One reason I consider him a hero is that he, perhaps more than anyone, helped the medical establishment begin to acknowledge that individuals can take an active role in the prevention of illness and in healing themselves.

My friend George DeSau deserves credit for being so unselfish with his knowledge and support.

I thank Kathy Ploof for all the typing and retyping that she did of this manuscript, as does Lori Scholten who spent many hours editing my early attempts at writing.

And there are so many others to thank including Bernie Siegel, Olga Worrall, Sister Giovanni, Norman Shealy, Carl Simonton, Jim Williams, Richard Herro, Curt Butters, Deloris Krieger, Bruce Iverson, Raymond Moody, and Marilyn Ferguson.

And finally, a special thanks to Warner Books Executive Editor, Joann Davis who asked me to write this book.

# CONTENTS

# CHAPTER 1

# POWERFUL STUFF!

*Money, which represents the prose of life,
and which is hardly spoken of in parlors
without an apology, is, in its affects and
laws, as beautiful as roses.*

Ralph Waldo Emerson

# You Can Rewrite Your Script

Perhaps, as Shakespeare said, the whole world is a stage and each of us are players or actors. If so, we have a tremendous advantage over the actors and actresses in plays: we can rewrite the script to our liking. We are not limited to our current script, which is based upon what we have accepted as "reality," or any subsequent script for that matter. In fact, before you have finished reading this book you will have written a new, more positive script for the rest of your life. But first you will:

1. Discover why you have been less financially successful than you'd like to be.

2. Learn how to eliminate the roadblocks to abundance.

3. Apply some powerful, easy-to-use strategies and techniques to attract money.

4. Improve self-image and self-esteem so you will maintain your wealth and enjoy a happier, more fulfilling life.

As we become more aware of what we really want, how to develop our potential, and how free we are to choose and achieve a happier, healthier, more successful life, then we can rewrite our script, and our life becomes pretty much as we have chosen it to be.

That you are reading this book suggests that your current script includes a state of financial lack—at least compared to your desires—that you would like to remove from your script, provided, of course, that doing so would not involve any painful or unwanted changes as well. I am happy to say that, on the contrary, the changes you will experience as a result of applying the strategies and techniques you are about to learn will be totally positive. You, and only you, will decide what your script will be; you will create a natural, more positive reality; and you will be more in control of your life than ever before.

## WHY SOME PEOPLE ATTRACT MONEY, AND OTHERS DON'T

Let's begin by looking at the main difference between people who attract well-above-average amounts of money and those who do not. The main difference (and often the *only* difference) is in the ways they think. This is not to say that people who attract money are more intelligent than the others. In fact there is no proof of any significant relationship between intelligence and prosperity.

Nor is the difference between wealthy people and those of modest means a matter of formal education. Although the average college graduate will earn much more than the average high school graduate, who, in turn, will earn more than the average dropout, there are countless exceptions. It is common knowledge that most self-made millionaires are not college graduates.

Is it just that some people are luckier than others? Yes, to some extent this is true. But as you will see later in this book, you can learn to create your own good luck. But it isn't just luck that separates those who become financially independent from those who struggle through life constantly in debt, barely able to make ends meet.

Again, the difference is in the ways we think, and our ways of thinking are based on the reality that we have accepted (usually very early in life, and usually at a subconscious level) that has us conforming to a life script brimming with false limitations. These false limitations prevent us from having and enjoying many things in life, especially large amounts of money. We have an idea of how much money we can "realistically" expect to earn and accumulate. We may indulge in wishful thinking about being more prosperous, but we don't really believe that it will ever truly happen. It just isn't part of our current script. We may even believe that it would be wrong or immoral for us to be wealthy. It may be okay for other people, but not for us. This kind of thinking is called *poverty consciousness.* Poverty consciousness leads to a condition of financial lack that is a continuing reality until these limiting beliefs are released and replaced with positive beliefs regarding money. This is known as *prosperity consciousness.*

Of course, people who are suffering from poverty consciousness are seldom aware of the limitations they have accepted and how these limitations have influenced their lives. The limitations are thoroughly accepted and believed to be reality. They believe that it is not within their power to change that reality, at least not without painful tradeoffs, such as having to give up time with family and friends, or sports, hobbies, and perhaps their health.

## The Purpose of This Book

The purpose of this book is to help you to: (1) become aware of the financial limitations you have accepted for yourself, (2) free yourself from false limitations, (3) decide what you *really* want, and (4) provide you with the tools and techniques to make it easy and natural for you to write your own script and to be prosperous and enjoy life more completely.

What you have here is a condensation of the most important things I have learned in the last twenty years about how to become financially independent, and enjoy it thoroughly. I started from nothing and accomplished this myself, and if you use the strategies and techniques offered in this book you can, too. And you'll enjoy some very pleasant "side effects" as well. You'll have a stronger, more positive self-image with high self-esteem, and you will enjoy better relationships and a happier, more fulfilling life. That's a promise!

## My Story

You will probably get more value from this book if I first tell you about myself and how I struggled early in life until I discovered the principles of prosperity that I am now happily able to share with you.

My first job after getting a degree from the University of Illinois was as an underwriter for an insurance company that paid me a whopping $375 per month.

A year or so later some friends of mine talked me into working with them in a business that involved theatrical productions. Although we eventually split up, I formed my own company and stayed in that business a few years, primarily promoting rock music concerts featuring popular disc jockeys and recording stars, and shows for children starring well-known television performers. This business provided a fairly good income, enabling me to support my wife and four children, but it was also very stressful and lacked the fulfillment I was seeking.

By this time I had read several books on positive thinking and motivation, but after reading each book, agreeing with the author, and getting all excited, I'd put the book down and go on doing things exactly as before. Reading these books didn't seem to help.

Then I encountered a course called Silva Mind Control. This program included techniques that helped me to internalize the positive thinking I had been reading about.

After a few months of training, I was teaching this program on weekends while running my other business during the week. I was doing so well with my classes that when offered the chance to be state director for this program in Minnesota, my wife and I talked it over and decided it would be a good move.

However, the royalty payments demanded by the Silva headquarters were so high that little profit was left to support my family. My income was getting smaller every month, and we were rapidly using up our savings. If business didn't get better we would have to sell our house. This was an especially difficult time for me because I had tied my sense of self-worth very much to being a good provider for my family. I have to admit I was scared! But as I'll emphasize later in this book, there is some good that comes with every hardship. What appears to be a very negative occurrence is often the best thing that could have happened—a blessing in disguise. It may take some time to realize what that blessing actually is, but after getting into the habit of looking for the positives or the lessons to be learned from what may at first seem to be totally negative events, it becomes much easier to recognize those blessings quickly. And soon you are automatically rewriting your script to include the likelihood of encountering these blessings.

The blessing in this instance was that I was forced by this inadequate income to become more creative in order to provide for my family. I developed a self-image and goal achievement workshop that supplemented the course I was teaching. The people who attended my self-image and goal achievement workshop loved it, and said it made what they had learned in the Silva program much more usable and valuable. Soon the Silva directors in Chicago, New York, Boston, Fort Lauderdale, and several other cities invited me to teach the workshop to their graduates, and those people loved it, too.

Unfortunately, after a year or so the Silva headquarters prohibited their instructors from sponsoring my workshop. Another "negative" occurrence for me.

And another blessing! It made it easy for me to learn and concentrate on expanding my workshop into a more comprehensive personal development program called Productive Meditation®. This new program I developed proved to be very effective, and the students said it was the best self-development program they had ever experienced. One of the most popular segments of this workshop dealt with developing a healthy attitude toward money. A prosperity consciousness.

Since I like to practice what I preach, I began using the prosperity strategies and techniques I was sharing, and which you will be learning shortly. I rewrote my life script to include financial independence. Although it took a while to see some positive changes, they eventually began to happen.

First, my classes became bigger and more profitable. Then I got ideas for conferences on health and mind development. I presented these conferences at the University of Minnesota and other colleges, and they were very successful. They featured world-famous people such as Buckminster Fuller, Norman Cousins, Olga Worrall, Bernie Siegel, Carl Simonton, Norman Shealy, Marilyn Ferguson, Joyce Brothers, Karl Menninger, Jerry Jampolsky, Lawrence LeShan, Delores Krieger, Raymond Moody, Wayne Dyer, and many others. Some of these illustrious people joined the board of advisors of my company, Effective Learning Systems, Inc., and I benefited tremendously from their knowledge and friendship.

By this time, my mind was truly open for greater financial success. I had rid myself of most of the negative programming I had accumulated over the years regarding money. By using the prosperity techniques I was teaching I had now prepared myself to be aware of opportunity when it comes knocking on the door, and how to differentiate between a real opportunity and something that on the surface may look or sound good but will lead to disappointment.

So there I was, positive, open-minded, well prepared by practicing what I was preaching, and along came a fine opportunity. It came when a good friend of mine, Curt Butters, informed me that he knew someone who had a mail-order business and was selling tapes by the thousands. Curt said, "These tapes are similar to yours, but yours are much better."

This news was very exciting to me. Up until that day I had been limiting my tape sales to people who had attended my workshops or university conferences. When

I became aware that the market was much more extensive, I jumped in with both feet. I just knew that this was a great opportunity and that I should proceed quickly, which I did.

The result? In the next several years I sold hundreds of thousands of my tape programs and have achieved financial independence. Equally important to me is that I have received many thousands of letters and phone calls from people who say the tapes have helped them to make positive changes in their lives. They had lost weight, quit smoking, improved memory, relationships, self-image, and so on.

It was better than a dream come true for me. I was doing something that was very important and satisfying to me: helping people develop their potential and live happier more successful lives. *And* I was earning more money than I ever dreamed was possible.

I feel very good about the money I have managed to attract. First of all, I earned it by providing good products and good services. Second, this prosperity has enabled me to help many more people than I was able to reach before. Third, I was free to try something I always had a desire to do, but didn't think I had enough time, money, or training to accomplish. I have recently written the words and music for two albums of songs. They are called *Songs for Self-Esteem* and they are for children (and the inner child in all of us). Writing these songs and having them published has been one of the most enjoyable, rewarding experiences of my life. And because I see a need for songs like these (difficulties in school, drug and alcohol abuse, crime, and other problems stem from low self-esteem) this work of love will probably produce a sizable profit.

# PUTTING MONEY TO GOOD USE

Money is a very important tool in this world, and I feel particularly good about how some of my students have used it. For example:

About twelve years ago Sister Mary Giovanni, who founded the Guadalupe Area Project (GAP) Alternative School in St. Paul, attended my classes and we quickly became good friends. She started the Guadalupe Area Project as a way of keeping troubled Hispanic students in school, and she was doing a great job, but she wanted to do more. At that time the school consisted of a small house, and the classrooms were so crowded she had to turn kids away. Kids who really needed another chance.

She learned my programming and goal-setting techniques, many of which are presented in this book, and became very excited about them. She asked if she could teach these techniques to her kids. So I gave her some tapes and printed materials and she repeated my class (about forty hours of training) and began teaching it at GAP. It was, and still is, known as the Effective Living class, and has helped many young people straighten out their lives and go on to college and good jobs.

One of the goals that Sister Giovanni wrote in my class was to raise enough money to build a much bigger school. Although this required a *very* large amount of money and some people told her it was an impossible goal, she refused to be discouraged, and soon she had not only built a fine new school, she also had the mortgage totally paid off.

Sister Giovanni was so pleased and excited by the techniques I shared with her she would often say with great enthusiasm, *"Wow! This is powerful stuff!"* She was right. It *is* powerful stuff. And it works!

It worked for Sister G., it has worked for me, and *it will work for you!* In fact, it should work even faster and better for you than it did for me because you won't have to dig and search and find out what's really effective through trial and error. It's all right here for you in this book.

Okay, you've read my little success story. Now let's get on with yours.

# CHAPTER 2

# CREATING A PROSPEROUS REALITY

*The mind is its own place, and in itself can make a heaven of Hell, a hell of Heaven.*

John Milton

William James said, "Human beings by changing the inner attitudes of their minds can change the outer aspect of their lives." When you change the inner attitudes of your mind to prosperity, you begin to attract money automatically. This change (prosperity consciousness) can be accomplished with the help of some easy-to-learn, easy-to-use strategies and techniques. By applying these strategies and techniques you will have the energy, ideas, attitudes, and motivation to rewrite your script and increase your income tremendously. You'll do it naturally, comfortably, and without the harmful stress you may have experienced in the past.

## PEACE OF MIND

I hasten to point out that the only true security is in having inner peace—a belief in your ability to adapt to changes and the acceptance and love for yourself and others. In other words, you must possess a well-rounded self-image with high self-esteem. Otherwise, even if someone were to give you a million dollars, you would not necessarily be financially independent. I know some millionaires who honestly will confide that they feel financially insecure. They have a poor self-image and actually, albeit unconsciously, find ways to lose their wealth. Or they may maintain their wealth but create other problems for themselves in areas such as health and personal relationships.

You hold the key to your own financial security. Using this key will not only bring you wealth but something far more valuable—peace of mind. This peace of mind can exist only in an atmosphere of loving acceptance for yourself and others. What a world of difference this would have made in the lives of Marilyn Monroe, Elvis Presley, and countless others who found wealth by itself was insufficient.

Therefore, we will proceed with a well-rounded approach to attracting money that focuses not only on how to accumulate wealth, but on doing what you love and what is purposeful for you. In the process you will discover and use your potential to enjoy better health, relationships, happiness, and success in all areas of life.

## Accept that it is "Morally Right" for You to Be Prosperous

Most people have allowed themselves to be programmed with financial limitations. They have acquired negative beliefs about money that have created a condition of lack. This is a negative reality wherein they are constantly, or almost constantly, lacking a sufficient amount of money to enjoy having the things they need or want and to do things they would like to do. For various reasons, they feel they do not "deserve" financial independence. They have acquired the belief that it may be all right for others to have wealth but not all right for them. In the past, some of them may have been taught that the Bible says, "Money is the root of all evil." This statement is not correct. What the Bible actually says is: "The *love* of money is the root of all evil."

Katherine Ponder, in her book *The Dynamic Laws of Prosperity*, says the Bible is a prosperity textbook. She writes that, "The very first chapter of the Bible describes the rich universe created for us and the last book of the Bible symbolically describes Heaven in rich terms."

Nevertheless, many people are not sure that it is spiritually right for them to desire prosperity. Obviously, money itself is not evil. It can certainly be used for evil purposes, but it can also be used in very positive ways—just as a hammer can be used to kill someone, it can also be used to build a home, church, or a school. Money can be a very useful tool. George Bernard Shaw said, "Money alone sets all the world in motion." Dostoevsky referred to money as "coined liberty."

Another reason many people are not sure that it is spiritually right for them to desire prosperity is that they may have the notion that there is only so much wealth in the world, and in order for them to have more it must be taken from someone else. This is a false assumption. As Buckminster Fuller often stated, "We have more than enough resources on this planet to raise the standard of living of *every human being* without reducing the standard of living of anyone." When we are using more of our potential, we become more creative, efficient, and productive, and we are better able to utilize the world's natural resources. We can produce goods and provide valuable services for one another. When this happens there are no losers. Everyone is a winner.

If you are constantly struggling to survive, you have less time and other resources to share with those around you. Only through overcoming the negative programming that has been passed to you, and has been passed from generation to generation, can prosperity be yours. During the Middle Ages, feudal systems assured wealth for just the privileged few. The teaching of "poverty and penance" was presented to the masses as the only road to salvation, so people could be kept in poverty. Privation was considered a "Christian virtue." Millions of people were misled into believing that to be poor was pious. This programming or conditioning helped to prevent the masses from rebelling, and it has continued through the centuries. Terms such as "filthy rich," "fat cat," and "rich bitch" illustrate this negative programming. That there is something wrong or immoral about attaining wealth were manmade ideas, not God's. A wealthy person can be just as virtuous as a poor person, if not more so, and that person's wealth can be used in many ways to benefit humanity. Being poor doesn't automatically make a person more spiritual than one who is prosperous. If this were the case we would not see so much crime and drug abuse in impoverished areas.

A negative attitude toward people merely because they are prosperous contributes heavily to a poverty consciousness. The more we resent the prosperity or success of others, the more we solidify our condition of poverty and lack of success. Such an attitude makes it almost impossible to attract money. A long time ago I began making a conscious effort to take joy in the good fortune and success of others. Why? Because I decided it was in my best interest to be happy for them and wish them continued prosperity.

Why was this in my best interest? For two reasons: (1) *Whatever we wish for others we attract to ourselves.* We keep the original, we just send out a copy. If we resent others for what they have and wish them misfortune, we tend to bring it unto ourselves. Harboring resentful thoughts and feelings toward others is not only a symptom of low self-esteem, the process itself causes great damage to our self-esteem. If we wish good things for others we tend to receive them ourselves. (2) *It enhances self-esteem.* I feel much better about myself when I am wishing others well rather than being "green with envy" and resentful. Consequently my self-esteem gets stronger when I am happy when other people experience good fortune. The higher our self-esteem, the more we allow ourselves to use our potential to achieve and maintain prosperity.

## BECOME AWARE OF NEGATIVITY

You actually have a choice. You can struggle as a slave to negative programming that creates poverty, or you can free yourself from it. How is this freedom accomplished? First, you must become aware of the negativity you are consciously and subconsciously experiencing, and recognize how this negativity has been influencing you. Then I will show you how to neutralize that negativity and replace it with positive thoughts, images, and feelings. This is accomplished by using programming techniques such as the Mental Movie in chapter 3 and/or the prosperity affirmations offered in this and subsequent chapters.

To some degree, negativity has influenced every phase of our lives. Negative thinking results in unhappiness, worry, anxiety, performance inefficiency, fears, depression, illness, and poverty. Many people use negatives automatically—never realizing what a devastating effect negatives are having on their lives.

The word *can't*, for example, has a permanent negative connotation. It's like saying, "This is the way it is and this is the way it always will be." And it will be, if you continue to say it. To borrow a thought from

Zig Ziglar, "Most of us could use a good kick in the can'ts."

Negative thoughts result in negative feelings or emotions—you become depressed. Whenever you feel "down" or moody, stop and ask yourself what you were thinking about just prior to your depressed mood. It will have been a negative thought.

Before you can develop prosperity consciousness, you must understand this negativity that has invaded your life. Why do you have these negative thoughts? Someone has taught or "programmed" you to accept negativity as a way of life. By accepting this negativity we have created limitations for ourselves, financially and otherwise, that exist only because of our acceptance of them. These limits do not represent our true potential. They are false limits and can be removed, but first we must become aware of them and how they arrived at such a position of power in our lives.

## Your Negative Programmers

### Parents

As a child, I was told by my parents, "Don't get your feet wet because you'll catch a cold." And sure enough, it would happen. I could get any other part of my body wet and have no problem, but if my feet got wet—*aahh-choo!*

The word *don't* is overused, especially when talking to children. If you call out to a child, "Don't slam the door," what is the next sound you are likely to hear? That's right—the door slamming. It is as if the child didn't hear the "don't." The result we get is from the positive part of the statement, "slam the door."

To illustrate this, I am going to ask you to do something. For the next thirty seconds, *don't think of a big, red apple!* If you are like most people, you did think of an apple. The *don't* did not seem to count.

Because children hear so many negatively stated commands, such as "Don't do that," "No-no," "Bad," and so on, they tune us out after a while. (This is also true of adults.) If you do not want the door slammed, you will get better results to say it in a positive way, such as "Close the door quietly, please."

Some of the money-related programming we received as children, besides the "spiritual" ones mentioned earlier are: "Money doesn't grow on trees," "We can't afford it," and "You'll never be rich."

## Other People

Frequently relatives, neighbors, friends, and co-workers act as your negative programmers. Sometimes their negative messages can have an immediate effect on your behavior. For example, have you ever met a friend and he or she immediately tells you how tired you look? Although you didn't feel tired before, you do now. Or have you ever been told, "Don't sit in a draft from an open window or you'll catch a cold"? You could play golf with the wind blowing at thirty miles an hour or ride a motorcycle at fifty-five miles per hour, and guess what? No cold.

What causes colds, anyway? We used to think it was a low temperature or drafts, but studies have shown that people can sit on kegs of ice in wind tunnels and not catch a cold. (Sound like fun?) We are also told that nutrition and rest will prevent us from having colds. However, there are some people who seem to receive proper nutrition and plenty of sleep, and they still have colds. Then, there are other people who receive what seems to be inadequate nutrition and little sleep, and they do not get colds. Could heredity be a factor? It could, but the case against heredity is weakened when people who frequently have colds suddenly stop having them and virtually never experience them again, after changing their beliefs about their susceptibility to them.

Now viruses are blamed for colds. But why does one person pick up these viruses and another person seem to avoid them, even when both people are constantly in the same environment, have similar nutrition, and get the same amount of sleep? Immunity or resistance is the likely answer. Or is it?

Could it be that a positive mental attitude can strengthen your resistance to illness? Based on my experience, the programming techniques that you will learn in this book definitely result in a mental outlook that strengthens your resistance. When I started to program to attract money, I remember thinking that I'd rather be healthy than wealthy. Of course! But where does it say I must choose between the two? This thought made me aware that I was programmed to believe that health and wealth were mutually exclusive. If I had one I couldn't have the other. What nonsense! And yet at a deep or subconscious level I believed it. I believed that if I were to gain wealth, I must lose my health. I vaguely recall that as a child I heard older people say I'd rather be healthy than wealthy. My assumption must have been that in order to be healthy it was necessary to forgo wealth. This, of course, is not logical, but much of our programmed limitations are terribly illogical. I don't know when or where I accepted this programming, but I am sure it played an important role in keeping me in a state of lack rather than prosperity.

## Television and Radio Commercials

Have you ever heard a radio or television commercial say, "When you get your next cold, try (product name)"? Think about that—"When *you* get *your* next cold." It is as if there were a cold with your name on it just waiting for you. (Incidentally, most people are possessive.) So if you have an ailment and say *"my* cold," *"my* asthma," *"my* ulcer," or *"my* headache," you are more likely to keep your cold, asthma, ulcer, or headache than if you say *"the* cold," *"the* asthma," and so on.

Here are some negative programming commercials to be aware of:

"The cold and flu season is here."

"There is a headache out there waiting for you."

"There are sixty-two pollens that can cause you hay fever; which one is yours?"

Sometimes commercials make the relief from illness so appealing that you can hardly wait until you do get "your" next cold so that you can try the drug. Or the commercial may show people getting a lot of loving care and concern when they are sick, suggesting that if we lower our resistance and become ill, we will receive the reward of love. The negative programming of commercials is a definite threat to your continued good health.

## Your Personal Negative Programmer—Yourself

Many years ago, someone told me that often our frequently used expressions can create physical problems for us. People who say "I can't see that" are more likely to have eyesight problems than those who do not say this. People who say "I can't stand that" are more likely to have problems with their feet than those who do not say this. People who say "I can't stomach that" are more likely to have ulcers than those who do not say this. And people who say "He gives me a pain in the ____," are more likely to have hemorrhoids than people who do not say this.

When I first heard that what we say can create some of our physical ailments, I rejected this idea immediately. Then I began to match expressions I had been using with my own physical problems. Could my ulcer be related to my "stomach" expression? I decided to play it safe and stop making such suggestions to my body. I believe that doing this must have made some difference because the ulcer disappeared. My advice is stop and listen to what you say. There could be a relationship between what you are *saying* and your *physical condition*.

## NEGATIVE STATEMENTS

The statements that follow are so common that it is easy to forget what a negative influence they can have on our mental, physical, and financial health, depriving us from achieving the success we desire. How often have you heard or said:

"I'll never be rich."
"Life is hard." (Compared to what?)
"I never get any breaks."
"I can't save money."
"That's too rich for my blood."
"It must be nice to have money." (Implication: I'll never have much.)
"Money is the root of all evil."
"He/she is *filthy* rich."
"Rich bitch."
"Money burns a hole in my pocket."
"Fat cat."
"I can never get ahead."
"I can't make ends meet."
"Money isn't everything."
"I'd have to work too hard to get rich."
"If I had money I'd just worry about losing it."
"If I earn a lot I'll just have to pay higher taxes."

"I hate my job."
"I hate selling."
"I'll never be able to _____."
"I can't afford to _____."
"I should have done _____."
"I think I was a brain donor at an early age."
"I'll never understand."
"It's impossible."
"All good things must come to an end."
"I'm no good at _____."
"I'm catching a cold."
"I'm losing my mind."
"Oh, my achin' back."
"I wish I were dead."
"You can't trust anyone."
"Just my luck."
"I'm dumber than a piece of wood."
"I'm falling apart."
"Bad news comes in threes."
"I'm a nervous wreck."
"I'm climbing the walls."
"I can't lose weight."
"I can't remember names."
"I'm always losing things."
"When you get old, your memory fails."
"That makes me sick."
"I forgot."
"You make me feel guilty."
"You make me angry."
"You make me unhappy."
"You made a fool of me."
"It's a dog-eat-dog world."
"If something can go wrong, it will."

And there are many more similar statements that people use every day, without a thought to what they are saying and doing to themselves. Let's look at a few of these statements more closely.

*"Bad news comes in threes."* This is a common statement often associated with death. So if two people that you know die, it is as if you are looking around for the third person to die. This statement has always made me uncomfortable. It is also used frequently in reference to business or financial problems. Why not, "Good news comes in threes"—or sixes, or tens, or more?

*"I can't remember names."* This statement is not only a negative—it is inaccurate, it is not so. All the people I've questioned who use this expression can remember their own name. So that's *one name*, at least. They can also remember the names of their family members, other relatives, friends, some people they work with; and their favorite recording artists, movie stars, television performers, athletes; and often their doctor, the president of the United States, and so on. When you get right down to it, they can probably remember hundreds and even thousands of names.

If you are dissatisfied with the way your memory has been functioning and you want to make a statement about this, it would be more accurate to say that "in the past I have not been too good at recalling names." But keep it in the past. That is where it belongs.

*"All good things must come to an end."* When we use this expression, we are usually thinking something bad is going to happen, and usually it does. Our expectancy creates it. Negative thinking and worry are so prevalent we tend to expect misfortune if we think we have been "too lucky." There are some folks who are very uncomfortable because "things have been going too well." Their belief is that this period of good times cannot continue. Unfortunately, these people are not even getting the full enjoyment of the good times, and the bad times will seem much worse than they really are.

This type of negative thinking can be reversed. No matter how bad things may be, it is helpful to think of your bad times as only a temporary condition. We can borrow from the Bible and say, "This, too, shall pass." Think of the times when things were not going well for you, and there was no end in sight; in fact, it looked as if it would just get worse and worse. But it didn't. Instead it got better, and would have done so sooner if you were expecting it and programming positively for it.

## How You Accept Negative Programming

After recognizing who your negative programmers are, you must understand your own internal process of accepting negativity into your life. You should know that I realize that during your life you were most likely also programmed positively with love. However, if you are like most of us, it seems that the negative messages outweighed the positive, especially in early childhood. To help you understand this internal process, a quick example of how you accept negativity is given first, then the steps of accepting negativity are discussed in detail, followed by an explanation of changing your reality.

As a young child, you had great potential and few limitations. And these limitations were usually conditions of childhood that you would eventually overcome, through such processes as growing and learning to walk, talk, read, and so forth. In those early years of your life, it was natural for you to think more in terms of possibilities, rather than impossibilities. However, since young minds are like sponges, if you were programmed negatively with great force, you tended to completely accept this negativity without question.

Often when a child does something naughty, a

parent will say, "You are a bad boy," instead of saying, "You did a bad thing." If the child hears the words "You are a bad boy" often enough, he will make the *assumption* that he truly is a bad boy. Then his *behavior* will begin to change, and he will start to act like a bad boy. When this behavior is sufficiently reinforced, the idea that he is a bad boy will become a *belief* with him. From then on he is hooked. His *life and reality have been formed*, and he grows into adulthood as a "bad boy" because his "bad boy" self-image had become real to him, and changed his reality.

## THE FOUR STEPS TO FORMING YOUR REALITY

**1.** *You make assumptions.* As you have probably guessed, most of the limitations that you have now are a result of the negative programming of your childhood. Because young minds are so receptive to outside stimuli, they quickly and easily make assumptions based on the input or programming from their environment. For example, you may have assumed older people (such as parents and teachers) were correct in their evaluation of you and the world around you. If they told you that something was impossible, you probably assumed that it could not be done. You also may have assumed, based on what you were told, that all people of a certain race or religion were bad, although you may never have met any of these people. You may have assumed that certain foods tasted terrible based on another person's statements regarding those foods. You may have assumed that these older people who were influencing you were appropriate behavior models for you, which was not always the case.

**2.** *Your behavior changes as a result of your*

*assumptions.* The assumptions you made influenced your thinking, feeling, and acting behavior. You began reinforcing the negative programming you received with your own internal dialogue (referred to in transactional analysis as replaying parent tapes), which damaged your self-image.

Other common behavior changes due to your assumptions include doubting, fearing, learning to hate, and difficulty in accepting and giving sincere compliments—no matter how well deserved. Your sense of self-worth begins to come more from the opinions of others, rather than from within yourself.

**3.** *Your behavior changes result in beliefs about yourself.* Your behavior encourages certain beliefs, which are more permanent than assumptions. Your assumptions may have led you to believe any or all of the following: "I am guilty"; "I should be perfect, and I'm not"; "I have definite limits"; "I am ugly"; "I am dumb"; "I am unlucky." Each of these beliefs then contributes to a general belief that "I am inadequate and undeserving of great happiness and abundance." The longer you believe something, the more firmly imbedded it becomes.

**4.** *Your belief becomes a reality for you.* Dr. Wayne Dyer's rewording of a familiar phrase describes this step. He says, "I'll see it when I believe it." Actually, this often happens very quickly. Suddenly all doubt has been removed, and you *know* the belief you have accepted is so. You know that the assumption, behavior, or belief that you have been experiencing is appropriate and correct ("I always knew I couldn't do it"; "they were right"). When you come to such a conclusion, the whole negative process is supported, and an inward spiral toward a more limited reality continues.

A graphic illustration of this process of creating is shown in figure 1. Our original reality in early childhood on the outside of the spiral is limitless. Then began the process of a limiting *assumption*, followed by a *behavior* change, leading to a *belief*, which forms our new, more limited *reality*. This new *reality* encourages more *assumptions* of limitations, which influence our *behavior*, creating an even more limiting *belief*, and so on. The spiral keeps moving toward realities that are more and more limiting, robbing us of the vast majority of our potential. As long as this process continues, we are missing out on much of the prosperity, happiness, peace, satisfaction, joy, adventure, excitement, health, love, and fulfillment of our lives.

## CREATING YOUR REALITY

You may have noticed that in the above paragraphs, the word *reality* is mentioned from time to time. What is your reality? Webster defines reality as "the quality or state of being real." It is a "real event, entity, or state of affairs" and the "totality of real things and events." So by "your reality" I mean what you as an individual experience or perceive as "real." What is real to me may not be real to you, and vice versa. And what was real to you as a child may no longer be real for you.

Many psychologists claim that we create our reality, and to a great extent I believe this is true. When we were infants, we had thus far acquired so little programming, information, or experience that there wasn't much to conflict with the messages that were sent to us, and became our assumptions. Therefore, any assumption, such as it being wrong for us to be wealthy, or that we'd never be rich, almost simultaneously became a belief and a reality for us. However, as we get older there is more resistance to anything that may be in conflict with our acquired programming, information, or experience. Consequently, it may take a longer time to create a new reality for ourselves than it did in early childhood, but it

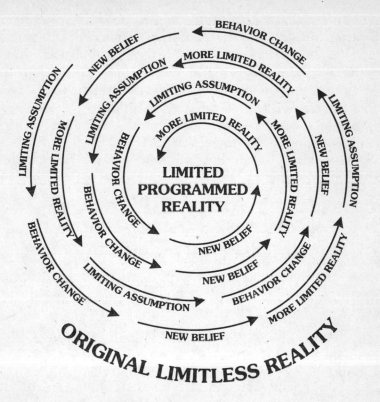

*Figure 1.* This inward spiral illustrates how our reality becomes more and more limited if we accept negative programming.

definitely can be done. I've done it, and I know thousands of people who are much healthier, wealthier, and happier because they have done it, too.

In other words, you make your own choices about how happy, healthy, and successful you are going to be, and what kind of relationships you have. One of the main points in Dr. Wayne Dyer's book, *Your Erroneous Zones,* is that we have the power to choose the things we want. When we acknowledge this power and consciously choose the way we want our lives to be, we have taken a big step toward being in charge of our lives.

You can choose to reject the negativity that bombards you, thus creating an unlimited reality. This is what you must learn to do now—neutralize your negative programming, choose to make more positive assumptions, and reverse the spiral that resulted in the limitations that are interfering with the acceptance of yourself as a person of unlimited potential who deserves to be prosperous.

## How to Reject Negative Programming, and Become a No-Limit Person

When you accepted your negative programming into your reality (see figure 1), you moved in a spiral from the unlimited reality of a child through the stages of limiting assumptions, limited beliefs, and finally, limited realities. You have moved closer to the center of this spiral, and in a state of limited programmed reality.

To reject (or neutralize) negative programming, you must reverse the spiral outward (see figure 2) from your limited programmed reality by choosing positive assumptions, which lead to positive changes in behavior, which help encourage more favorable assumptions, and so forth. Gradually you overwhelm your programmed limitations with new realities, and you become a no-limit person. Eventually, through expanding your consciousness and awareness, you continue to evolve, learn, grow, improve, and utilize your true potential for happiness and success. This expansion of your consciousness and awareness can occur only when you understand how to reject negative programming—or you understand how to clear out the garbage in your thinking.

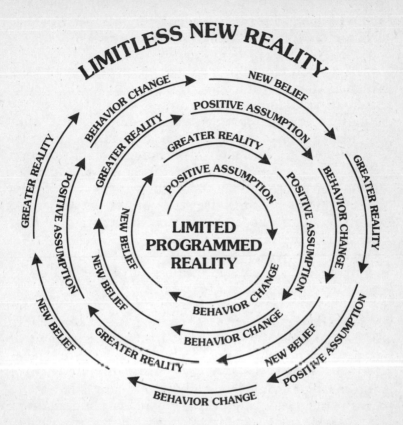

*Figure 2.* This outward spiral illustrates the process of freeing yourself from false limitations to become a no-limit person.

# THE SIX STEPS OF REVERSING YOUR SPIRAL

**1.** *Recognize your negative programming.* The first step to neutralize negativity is to be aware of it. When you are talking or thinking in negative terms, or receiving it from someone else, let it be like a red light flashing, or a bell ringing, or a siren blaring within you.

This will put you on mental alert, and remind you that your mental computer is being programmed.

**2.** *Neutralize the negative and replace with a positive.* If you choose not to let negative programming influence your life in a negative way, press the CLEAR button in your mind, as you would on a calculator or computer if you had just pressed a number or letter that you did not want registered. Then, mentally replace the negative thought with a positive thought, or affirmation, just as on a calculator you would replace the number you did not want with another number. This would also be the same as pressing the EJECT button on your tape player to replace a tape that you no. longer want to hear with a more desirable recording.

The following affirmations, or success statements as I like to call them, have proven to be very helpful when used immediately after clearing or ejecting a negative thought or statement. It is also recommended that you write down those success statements that you believe will be most helpful for you and get into the habit of repeating them many times each day. As you are repeating them, allow yourself to feel the appropriate positive emotions that would normally accompany such statements if they were being made by you as a statement of fact. Let yourself experience the feelings of elation, confidence, satisfaction, power, energy, enthusiasm, or other positive emotions.

**The success statements are:**

❑ **I choose to be wealthy.**

❑ **I choose to be successful.**

❑ **Financial independence is mine.**

❑ **I project wealth and good fortune to each person I meet. By doing this, I turn my** consciousness toward the inexhaustible, Universal Source of abundance.

❏ When I project wealth and good fortune to others, I benefit myself.

❏ When I increase another person's prosperity consciousness, I increase my own.

❏ I teach best what I most need to learn, and it returns to me from many directions.

❏ Money is my friend.

❏ I'm comfortable having money.

❏ I now see myself as a prosperous person.

❏ Large amounts of money are coming to me.

❏ Money flows to me easily and naturally, just as the waves flow into a shore.

❏ Regardless of the state of the economy, my financial condition continuously improves.

❏ I deserve great sums of money and use it to help myself and others.

❏ I am putting more loving energy into my work, and this is providing me with a larger and larger income.

❏ The more money I have, the more money I have to share.

☐ **My financial worth increases every day, regardless of what I do. Money is always circulating freely in my life, and there is always a surplus.**

☐ **I am learning and growing every day, which increases my value to the world.**

☐ **Every dollar I spend circulates, enriches the economy, and comes back to me multiplied.**

☐ **Every day I am prospering. Every day my wealth is multiplying.**

☐ **I am advancing and growing in wealth and wisdom.**

☐ **I see money as a useful tool.**

☐ **The more money I have, the more money I have to use to help myself and others.**

☐ **I will always be prosperous because I have an intense desire to contribute to humanity and all of life.**

For some people, just repeating a few of these statements with *feeling* many times daily, as directed above, is all it takes to enable them to become independently wealthy. You may be one of those people.

It may be that easy for you. In that case you could stop reading here and just use your success statements. However, what follows is extremely valuable and will further assure your financial success and peace of mind.

But you can and should start using your success state-ments *today.* The sooner you do, the sooner you'll have the prosperity you are seeking.

Always remember that you can take control. You are responsible for your thoughts, and you can create any reality you desire. So use the CLEAR or EJECT button, whichever you prefer, and start taking charge of your life. This will weaken past negative programming, and help you rid yourself of false limitations.

It could be that there are no limitations at all. Perhaps there are some things humans will never be able to do, but I believe that someday much of what we currently think is impossible will be easily accomplished. Scientists agree that we use only a small percentage of our brains. When you clear out the garbage that robs you of your mental talents and you decide to control the programming that goes into your mental computer, you will think in terms of possibilities instead of impossibil-ities, and free yourself to use more of your potential.

**3.** *Make the positive into an assumption.* When you make a positive assumption, it is important to understand that assumptions are not the same as beliefs. You can assume almost anything for a limited time. Also, it is easier to make an assumption than to estab-lish a full-fledged belief.

**4.** *Your behavior changes as a result of your posi-tive assumption.* Your positive assumption automati-cally influences your behavior, and you are moved to action. The behavior will continue if it acquires energy such as experienced in the process of positive visualiza-tion that you'll learn in the next chapter, or positive feedback such as an immediate good result. Be your own best friend at this stage, and give yourself positive support.

**5.** *Your behavior changes result in a new belief.* For this to happen, it is critical that the behavior change last long enough for the belief to become established. Then you begin to believe new, positive thoughts.

**6.** *Your positive belief becomes a reality for you.* You are now moving to outward, unlimited reality on the spiral. You have completed the process of positive thinking. Many people do not understand this process because either (1) they have not learned to program themselves properly (much of this book is devoted to helping you do just that), (2) they give up too easily (persistence is covered in a later chapter), or (3) they are not neutralizing the negativity they encounter.

## EXAMPLES OF USING THE POSITIVE SPIRAL PROCESS

*Making Friends More Easily.* The ability to make friends easily is extremely valuable to us in both business and social life. In this example, I am assuming that you have no negative programming to clear. Then you can make friends more easily by first *assuming* that the person you have just met or are about to meet is a friendly, warm, sensitive, loving, and lovable human being who has many fine qualities, some of which may not be immediately evident. You further assume that you will like each other.

These *assumptions* automatically influence your *behavior* in that the things you say, how you say them, your body language, and your thoughts are more positive and conducive to an amicable relationship.

Your actions or *behavior* strengthen your assumption to the point of *belief.* You actually believe what you have chosen to assume about this person—who by this time is mirroring your positive assumptions and behavior. Consequently, your belief is supported by your experience, and becomes your *reality.* Now you find that wherever you go, you can surround yourself with people you can enjoy. In a sense, you are creating those people as you create your reality.

*Creating the Reality of Being Prosperous.* You begin by assuming you were *meant* to be wealthy. It is your birthright. It is morally right for you and the conditions are perfect for you to become financially independent. Pressing the CLEAR or EJECT button on negatives and using some of the following success statements will help you make this assumption and help carry you through the spiral to your unlimited reality.

- ❏ **I deserve to be wealthy.**

- ❏ **I was meant to be prosperous.**

- ❏ **I am like a magnet to money—I attract it.**

- ❏ **Money flows to me easily and effortlessly.**

- ❏ **I use my rapidly increasing wealth to help myself and others.**

This *assumption* automatically influences your thinking, feeling, and acting *behavior*. You set some financial goals. You become more aware of opportunities and begin to take advantage of those opportunities. Your energy level increases, and you become more enthusiastic, positive, and active. This behavior causes you to *believe* that you are destined to be more prosperous and it becomes your reality even before you have actually attained great wealth. At this point you have gone beyond merely believing. You *know* you are prosperous. Conrad Hilton was once asked when it was that he realized that he was truly wealthy. Mr. Hilton replied, "I realized it when I was sleeping on park benches." He *knew* he was successful, even then. Reality starts in the mind. You must see it and feel it within you. That "inner reality" will produce your physical reality.

*Creating the Reality of Being a Successful Sales-person.* If you are in sales or are considering a business or position that involves selling a product, service, or idea, you will find it extremely helpful to overcome any negative programming you may have regarding selling. Many people have an aversion to selling because they believe it involves imposing upon people, taking advantage of them, or making them spend money for something they don't need or want. They also are afraid of rejection or failure. It may take a little soul-searching for you to become aware of this negative programming within you. When you determine what this negative programming is—or become aware of it—then you must push your CLEAR button. At that point you must immediately *assume* that you already are a good salesperson. To help you make this assumption use success statements such as:

- ❑ **I enjoy selling.**

- ❑ **When I am selling, I am providing a good service.**

- ❑ **I love to show people how my product can help them.**

- ❑ **I do my buyers a favor by calling, and I enjoy giving.**

- ❑ **Selling is now fun for me.**

- ❑ **I am good at selling.**

This *assumption* automatically influences your behavior, and you are moved to action. (Perhaps you make more calls, become more enthusiastic about your product or service, or become more sensitive to your customers needs and desires, and how your product or service can meet those needs and desires.) This *behavior* begins to open the channels to new energy and leads to a true *belief* that you are a successful salesperson, and it may become a *reality* for you even before it is supported by your experience.

## ESTABLISH A MINIMUM LEVEL OF PROSPERITY

You know by now that in the past you have accepted false limitations that contained your ability to attract, keep, and enjoy money to the fullest. And you've probably already begun to free yourself from those false limitations and move outward on your spiral to the unlimited reality of abundance and happiness.

However, you may find it helpful to accept at least one limitation. Namely that your financial condition will *always* remain above a certain minimum that you choose. In other words, choose a level of wealth below which you will never go. If you accept this minimum amount as a limitation, just as most people have accepted limitations on the level of prosperity they can achieve, you will somehow find a way (legally and painlessly) to remain above that minimum level. Why? Because if you accept as "reality" that you will always remain above that minimum level, you provide yourself with a "wake-up call" to direct your inner mind to provide you with the ideas, motivation and greater awareness of opportunities that will enable you to remain above that minimum level. Even if you experience a temporary downturn, your energy, motivation and creativity will be automatically activated to enable you to attract more money, regardless of the circumstances.

This is not the same as viewing that minimum as the "right" level for you, for that would be accepting a limitation that would prevent you from enjoying a much higher degree of prosperity.

This is just a way of assuring yourself that your success won't lead you to become so complacent that you fall asleep at the switch and allow temporary setbacks to become permanent.

It's a little like having a sell order on a stock to protect your profits. Even the most prosperous people in the world experience bad breaks, but as the saying goes, when the going gets tough, the tough get going. Your positive limit serves as a wake-up call to activate your energy and creativity when you need it. As Robert Schuller says, "Tough times never really last, but tough people do."

As you will see in chapter 6, obstacles or setbacks are often blessings in disguise. We can learn from them and, as a result, become even more successful than we would have been had we never encountered that obstacle or "bad break."

In this chapter you have learned:

1. To accept that it is morally right for you to be prosperous.

2. To become aware of negative programming and how it starts you spiraling toward a "reality" of false limitations.

3. How to neutralize (CLEAR or EJECT) negative programming and replace it with success statements that move you outward in the spiral toward unlimited reality and your true potential for health, happiness, and prosperity.

4. To establish a minimum level of prosperity.

In the next chapter you will learn a very powerful visualization technique that will make it even easier to move outward on your spiral to financial independence and a more positive, fulfilling life.

# CHAPTER 3

# SUCCESS
# THROUGH
# VISUALIZATION

*Whatever your mind can conceive and believe, it can achieve.*

Napoleon Hill

Have you ever read or heard people say: "You become whatever you hold in your mind"? Of course, this is not *literally* true, for if it were then many men I know would be women, and vice versa. Perhaps a better way to put it is that what we dwell upon in our minds becomes our physical reality.

Everything begins in the mind. Even books are merely records of what has already happened in someone's mind. The universe itself could be thought of as stemming from a thought in the mind of God. The things we see about us every day, such as furniture, clothes, appliances, telephones, houses, cars, airplanes, all were real in someone's mind before they became physical realities.

Because we can create much of our reality, if not all of it, with our thoughts, why not choose to create a more positive reality in all realms of life? *We can create the success we desire by directing the thoughts and images and feelings in our mind.*

As a matter of fact, we are all 100 percent successful right now. If we've been holding thoughts, images, and feelings of success in our minds, we've been successful at being successful. And if we've been holding thoughts, images, and feelings of failure in our minds, we've been successful at being failures. Most of us have experienced mixed results so far, due to our mixture of positivity and negativity. Sometimes we are pleased with our realities, and sometimes we are displeased. The results are due to the ways we positively and negatively program ourselves and the positive and negative programming we accept from others.

## Everything We Experience Is Programming

The research of Dr. Wilder Penfield, a neurosurgeon at McGill University in Montreal, illustrates how brains can be programmed. Dr. Penfield discovered during brain surgeries that if he touched the temporal cortex with a weak electric probe, the patients would recall prior events— things that happened to them many years before, events they thought they had forgotten. They not only recalled these events but also relived them, experiencing a dual awareness. They knew they were in surgery (a local anesthetic was used so the patients could respond to the instructions of the surgeon), and yet they were also back in time reexperiencing an event.

Penfield says that everything we experience in our conscious awareness is recorded on our brain cells. It is more or less like a videotape recording, only with emotion, with feeling. And we don't need an electric probe to trigger the replaying of these events. It can happen to us in our daily lives. For example, if we hear a song that has emotional significance for us, we may suddenly find ourselves back in time reliving or reexperiencing the thoughts and feelings we had when we previously heard that song.

Sometimes we may feel depressed, or fearful, or lack confidence, even though we have no logical reason to feel that way. We just do. Nevertheless, such feelings can control or program our self-image and behavior. Everyone has a very large collection of recordings; some are positive and some are negative. In chapter 2 you learned how to neutralize past negative programming. You have also learned to use affirmations to create positive recordings.

You are now about to learn a method that is even more effective than affirmations for programming yourself with positive thoughts, images, and feelings, and for creating your reality. This programming method will help you to use more of your potential and to consistently achieve your desired results, whether they involve money, relationships, health, sports, school, business, or whatever. It is called the Mental Movie.

## THE MENTAL MOVIE

The Mental Movie method involves all of your senses: sight, sound, smell, touch, taste, and even your intuitive senses. You will create two imaginary reels of film: one for the present situation, and one for the end results you desire. Here is how to play the Mental Movie:

1. Begin by taking three deep breaths. Hold each for a few seconds, and while exhaling say to yourself, "Relax." This helps you to calm your mind so you can more easily reprogram it with positive thoughts, images, and feelings.

2. Imagine you are in a projection room. There is a projector, a screen, and film. It is set up just for you. Someone may be operating the projector for you, or you may be doing it yourself.

3. The film with the present situation is projected on the screen. Immediately you may see the situation with new perceptions. Observe your thoughts and feelings during this process. Make a mental note of any insights.

Because you are in complete control at all times, you may stop the film at any point or replay any part for better comprehension. You feel comfortable, open, understanding, and perceptive. You view this as an opportunity to learn and grow.

While using this first reel you may become aware of programming and/or choices that may have helped to create the present situation. You needn't try hard to make these discoveries, just make a mental note if they come to your awareness.

4. Change reels when you are ready. Usually a few minutes is sufficient. Now project the multidimensional movie of the desired end result. Involve all your senses. Feel and enjoy the desired end result. It is not something you are merely wishing or hoping for—it is already happening, and you are enjoying it thoroughly. Dwell on this desired end result for thirty to sixty seconds.

Step inside that movie and be a part of it. Let it be as real as wherever you are and whatever you are experiencing at this moment—as real as anything you have ever experienced. Allow yourself to be totally surrounded by the positive end result, enjoying it thoroughly. Involve all your senses—sight, sound, smell, touch, taste, even your intuitive senses. Allow yourself to experience the positive feelings that go along with this end result. Feel the confidence, satisfaction, fulfillment, joy—all the rewards that are associated with this positive end result.

5. Now release that end result. Relax, for the programming is completed. You have planted the seeds.

The first reel is automatically stored away and will never be replayed, unless you consciously decide to reexamine the problem situation. All programming for this project in the future will involve the desired end result only. Therefore, you will give energy to the solution rather than to the problem. The more emotion you put into the programming, the more the positive emotion you feel when doing this, the more powerful the programming. If we have a negative or traumatic experience in our childhood, we can go back and replay it over and over again throughout our lives. It can literally control our lives. Likewise, a positive experience can come back and be played over and over again, and that is exactly what will happen if we dwell on positive thoughts, images, and feelings in a relaxed state of mind. Those feelings of satisfaction and fulfillment, of confidence and enjoyment can be automatically replayed anytime.

The Mental Movie makes it more likely for us to automatically experience these positive feelings over and over again in many different situations in the future. After using this technique for a while you'll probably notice yourself feeling very positive and confident without even trying. And when we feel confident and positive, we seem to function more effectively in everything we do. This helps us to tap our energy and we are better able to use more of our potential.

If distracting thoughts occur during your programming, this is perfectly normal. Just brush those thoughts gently aside and bring your mind back to where you want it to be. Each time you do this you go deeper, you become stronger with more control. (You will notice that when you are focusing on the positive end result and you're feeling the satisfaction, fulfillment, enjoyment, and so forth, that your mind is less likely to wander. The positive emotions help you to concentrate and focus on what is most important to you at that moment.)

## When to Use the Mental Movie

The best time to use the Mental Movies is just prior to going to sleep. Our dreams and the quality of our sleep are influenced by our thinking just before we fall asleep. Using the Mental Movie will cause positive and creative dreams and more restful and productive sleep. You may wake up in the morning with a solution to a problem, a creative idea, or you may find it easier to make a decision that seemed difficult for you to make the night before.

The next best time to program is the first thing in the morning. This will reinforce your previous evening's programming and give you a good start on an enjoyable, productive day. Wake up a few minutes earlier than usual in order to do this. Those few minutes of programming will energize you, making you feel as though you had hours of additional sleep. This extra energy usually lasts the entire day.

Keep in mind that after your initial programming for any project, all programming will involve the desired end result only. When you program for it in the future, you need only dwell on that positive end result for a half a minute to a minute, and then release it. Let it go. And realize you've planted the seeds, and they are in there working for you. Since you need only dwell on the end result for thirty to sixty seconds, you will have time to program for five or six things in five minutes.

## USING THE MENTAL MOVIE FOR FINANCIAL SUCCESS

You can use your Mental Movie technique to program for prosperity. Just relax your mind the usual way and run the film of the situation as it now exists. Allow yourself to become aware of the facts and to calmly study the situation in this relaxed state of mind. Be aware of the programming you have received that has contributed to the situation. Also be aware of choices you have made to help bring about the present situation.

Looking at it from different angles, make a mental note of any insights you gain from studying the problem at this dimension. If distracting thoughts occur, this is perfectly normal, just brush them gently aside and bring your mind back to where you want it to be. Each time you do this you go deeper, become stronger, with more control.

When you feel that you've spent enough time with this reel, lock it up, and put on the reel of the positive end result (the situation as you would like it to be). Allow yourself to mentally project forward to a point in time where your goal is realized. It is already happening. Let yourself feel the reward of having achieved this desired end result. Allow yourself to experience the appropriate emotions that go along with this positive end result. Enjoy the confidence, the happiness, the satisfaction, the fulfillment. Allow the positive feelings to build, and enjoy the sensations.

Imagine money flowing to you easily and naturally. Imagine seeing large amounts before you. You can feel it in your hands. Allow yourself to experience complete financial independence and enjoy the power this gives you to make positive changes in this world. Picture yourself using this money very effectively to help yourself and others to enjoy life and to help make this world a better place in which to live. You are walking, talking, standing, sitting, and feeling as a wealthy, healthy, confident, successful person. You choose this as the inner image of yourself. All thoughts are creative. Each thought you have contributes to your future reality. You are creating your future reality. Whatever the mind can conceive and believe, it can achieve.

After spending about a minute dwelling on these positive end results, release the goal image and just relax and enjoy, knowing that you've planted the seeds and you will soon reap the benefits at the physical dimension. Remember, the more positive emotion you allow yourself to feel, the less your mind will wander, and the easier it will be for you to visualize and focus on the desired end results. This programming accumulates; the more you do it, the more you will control and enjoy your future.

## PROGRAMMING FOR A BETTER JOB

Many people have successfully used the Mental Movie to program for a better job. Here are some suggestions for using it for that purpose: If you are seeking employment with a new organization or company, before applying for a job it is wise to find out as much about your prospective employer as you can. This will help you to determine if it is a good place for you to work. Find out what products or services this company offers. You can often get this information from the librarian at your public library, from a friend, relative, or acquaintance who works for that company, or from the company itself. If it is a publicly held company, a stockbroker can send you information on that company that is made available for potential investors.

Once you have decided that you want a particular job, you can begin using mental imagery and positive emotions to help make this a reality. Begin by calming your mind using three deep breaths. Then run the first reel and examine the situation as it now exists. Study it from different angles. Be aware of the choices that may have contributed to the situation. Also be aware of the programming that may have contributed to the present situation.

After you've spent what you feel is sufficient time examining the situation as it now exists—and this may be just a few minutes—then put that reel away and lock it up. Then project the reel with the positive end result. Once again allow yourself to feel the satisfaction, the fulfillment, the confidence, all the appropriate positive emotions. Put yourself into that movie, involve all your senses, and enjoy it thoroughly. See yourself having the job you desire. Be as specific as you can be about the job. If you want to be office manager or sales manager or foreman or president of the company, see yourself in that job. Feel yourself already there: walking, talking, acting, thinking, feeling like the person you choose to be. In your mind you already have that job, and you are performing it very effectively.

After enjoying this positive end result for about one minute, release it and realize that you have planted the seeds for a better job.

The more real it is at this inner dimension, the sooner it becomes reality at the outer dimension. Everything begins in the mind, so you must create that reality within, and it will be reflected in everything you do. You will show more confidence in yourself. Those in charge of hiring are more favorably impressed with people who seem confident than those who do not. If you are seeking a promotion from your current employer, those in charge of promotions will sense your confidence and recognize that you are ready to move up, and you will get the promotion sooner.

If you are in business for yourself or if you are in sales, people you do business with are going to sense if you have confidence in your product or service. People like to do business with those who have confidence in themselves and their product or service. This must begin within. You can be phoney, but you can only fool people so far with that phoniness. If you have true confidence, it will be part of everything you do: the way you talk, the way you walk—everything. You will have an aura of confidence. Your tone of voice, your smile, your posture, and all of your body language will be influenced by that confidence. Create that reality in your mind, and it will soon be your physical reality as well.

## USING THE MENTAL MOVIE FOR A JOB INTERVIEW

Often people who are very well qualified fail to get the job they seek because they don't make a good impression in the job interview. Here is how to mentally rehearse for success in that situation. This too is done by first taking three breaths, and each time while exhaling saying the word "relax," and then visualizing yourself enjoying a successful interview. You arrive for the interview a few minutes early. You have a neat, well-groomed appearance. You are fully prepared with the facts of your work history, your school and/or your service record, your interests, your plans, your aspirations. You are also prepared to talk about your achievements as a member of organizations or teams.

You greet your interviewer with a firm handshake and wait until you are asked to be seated. You make brief eye contact with the interviewer and mentally project, "I love you." Though these words are spoken silently, it helps you to make a good first impression because it allows you to feel more relaxed, more comfortable, more confident. It helps you to be more natural and spontaneous, more animated and enthusiastic. It helps you to be the real you. And when people are being themselves, they make a better impression than when they are inhibited or putting on an act. Projecting "I love you" may also cause you to speak with a more pleasant tone of voice, and smile a little more easily, which also helps to make a good impression.

People tend to mirror what you project. If you're

smiling and projecting love, they are likely to do the same. It also helps to think the following thoughts: "There is something about this interviewer that I like very much. I may not know at this moment what that something is... but I know I like this person. I feel good being with this person." Feel yourself projecting love and feeling more confident and natural. You are more at ease, which allows your sense of humor to become more evident. You are giving clear and reasonably rapid responses to questions, and you are projecting yourself as a warm, intelligent person.

You are focusing on your assets, on what you have to offer the company, such as honesty, dedication, skill, knowledge, experience, creativity, desire to learn and contribute, the ability to work well with others, loyalty, and the fact that you enjoy working on a team to accomplish something. You are expressing to the interviewer why you want to work for that company, and why you want that particular job. You find it easy to express why you think you are the right person for that job. Keep focusing on your assets you have to offer, and projecting love.

In your mind, see your interview going exactly the way you want it to go. Allow yourself to experience the positive emotions that accompany this end result. Feel the confidence, joy, enthusiasm, the sense of strength, energy, and inner peace—whatever to you means that the interviewer is favorably impressed with you and your qualifications.

You feel comfortable asking questions about the details and responsibilities of the job, about additional training that may be necessary, and about opportunities for advancement.

You will find it rewarding and enjoyable to relax your mind and dwell on a successful interview at least three times a day. This will help you to be more comfortable and confident, and make a very favorable impression.

## THOUGHT CONDITIONERS

Norman Vincent Peale has written a little book entitled *Thought Conditioners*. In this booklet he takes passages from the Bible and gives his interpretation of these passages. Each one is arranged so you can tear it out of the book and carry it around with you in your wallet or purse. Here are two of my favorite "Thought Conditioners":

**The Magic of Asking and Believing:**
**"Ask and it shall be given you, seek and ye**
**shall find, knock and it shall be**
**opened unto you."**

(Matthew 7:7)

Dr. Peale says, "This is a very practical technique of prayer. It works amazingly. One reason we do not get answers to our prayers is that we ask but we do not really expect to receive. We are expert askers, but inexpert receivers. This spiritual formula tells us to ask and then immediately conceive of ourselves as receiving. For example, to be free from fear ask the Lord to free you. Then believe immediately that he has done so. The minute you express your faith by asking him for a blessing and believe your prayer has been answered, your prayer is answered."

People of all religions report that prayers work, and after surveying hundreds of clergymen and women whom I have had in my classes, along with thousands of laypersons, I can state that those who are getting the best results from prayer are using this approach. The way I used to pray was very negative. I would ask for something and immediately begin thinking, "I don't deserve it," or, "It probably won't happen." Guess what? I was usually right.

Although I had become cynical, almost giving up on prayer, I found that my programming was often also praying—a positive way of praying. Incidentally, I have noticed that programming helps many people develop their spirituality.

Belief is an important element in programming. The more you believe it is so, the more powerful your programming will be. William James, considered the father of American psychology, stated, "Our belief at the beginning of an undertaking is the only thing that insures the successful outcome of our venture." Another helpful verse of scripture is Mark 9:23 "... if though canst believe, all things are possible to him that believeth."

*Freedom from Fear:*
**Another helpful Thought Conditioner from Norman Vincent Peale deals with conquering fear. "The thing which I greatly feared is come upon me, and that which I was afraid of has come unto me."**

(Job 3:25)

Dr. Peale says, "This Thought Conditioner states a very serious warning. If, over a long period of time, a person habitually fears something, there is a tendency for that fear to become a reality. For example, if you fear you are going to fail and you constantly entertain thoughts of failure, you'll create a mental condition that is propitious to failure. Creative, positive, success factors are repelled by your mind because your mind is filled with defeat attitudes. On the contrary, if you hold a faith thought, a positive thought, you will create about yourself an atmosphere propitious to success, health, and well-being."

Fear definitely influences our behavior. Most people would have no problem walking on a board ten inches wide if it were only ten inches above the ground or suspended between two chairs. However, if the same board were suspended between two tall buildings, the fear of falling would make it very difficult.

Many years ago, my fear of skin problems helped to create a skin disease. My fear of being disliked created self-consciousness. My fear of being nervous created nervousness. My fear of slicing a golf ball created slices. My fear of catching a cold lowered my resistance to colds. My fear of financial problems created financial problems.

Think about it. Maybe you have created through fear some of the negative things you have experienced. I am convinced that I created negative happenings in my life out of fear. Using the Mental Movie helped me to overcome such fears, and to move outward on the spiral to much more positive and successful realities.

## CREATIVITY AND PROGRAMMING

When you are using the Mental Movie and you are in a relaxed state of mind focusing on positive end results, you are tuning in to the Universal Source of creativity. Thus, ideas will often come to you about what you actually can do to bring about those positive end results. Perhaps you have tried hard to get those ideas before, and they escaped you, but suddenly here they are. You projected forward in time, and now have the benefit of hindsight.

Hindsight makes it easy to look back and say how it should have been, like telling the football coach on Monday what he should have done on Sunday. Seeing the results in advance isn't as easy, unless you use the Mental Movie. The creative people throughout history—inventors, discoverers—were dreamers; all imagined how things could be. They projected to that end result, enjoyed it, and then the ideas would come.

You may wish to look at it this way. Suppose you knew there was a huge treasure chest filled with cash, gold, and diamonds one hundred feet in front of you and it is all yours if you can reach it in five minutes. But you must find your way through a maze to get to it. And you are not sure of which path to take. You may become so immobilized with fear of selecting the wrong path that you may do nothing at all and you get nowhere. Or you could start out on a path and then begin to doubt if it is the right path and back off and then try another path and do the same thing. Once again you get nowhere. But when you use the Mental Movie method of programming, it is as if you've moved forward in time and you are already at the end of the maze. And at the location of the treasure you are at an elevated position and can look out and see the path that leads to that treasure, and then you can come back to that point in time where you started and you know which path to take.

In one of my classes, a scientist with one of the world's largest corporations, a great inventor, shared an example of this process from his personal experiences. He said, "I would be trying very hard to invent a machine and was getting nowhere until I finally started to fantasize. I would pretend I had already invented the machine and I would be very happy about it. I would be playing with it like a child plays with a toy. I would be showing it to friends, and explaining it to colleagues. In the process of doing this, ideas would come to me on how I could put such a machine together. And then I was able to do it." He discovered how important it is to mentally project forward in time, get to the desired end result, and enjoy it. Doing so triggered his creativity.

I used to try very hard to be creative. I would be frustrated because my creative friends were always coming up with ideas. I felt inadequate and uncreative because ideas were few and far between for me. No matter how hard I tried, I made very little progress.

Once I became very determined, deciding, "Boy, I'm going to do it. I know somewhere in there I've got good ideas and I'm going to get them out." So I'd set aside some time when the conditions would be ideal, when there would be no distractions, and I would say to myself, "This time the ideas will come." Then I'd sit down (with pencil, paper, and tape recorder, ready for action), try very hard, and just draw a blank. Nothing would come; consequently, I would become even more frustrated and disgusted with myself and decide that I just was not creative.

Sometime later, after learning about programming, I decided to dwell on a positive end result: attracting more money. I was not trying to get ideas, but I believed that somehow magically my financial condition would improve if I followed this process. While enjoying the positive end result, and not straining, forcing, wishing, or even hoping, but imagining I already had the money, I began to wonder how I had arrived at this end result. Then it suddenly became apparent what could be done to bring about that end result. The ideas that were escaping me before were suddenly there.

The doors to creativity seem to open and ideas

start to flow in when we are focusing on positive end results in a relaxed state of mind. Sometimes while doing this, the ideas will come in so fast that it will be difficult to keep track of them.

## Using the Mental Movie to Motivate Yourself

In addition to stimulating your creativity, the Mental Movie is also a great tool for self-motivation. When you allow yourself to experience positive end results in a relaxed state of mind, you will find yourself getting so enthusiastic and confident about creating that reality in your physical world that you can hardly wait to get started. This enthusiasm and confidence increases your energy level, and whatever has to be done to bring about that physical reality doesn't even seem like work. It is fun.

Although there may be some sacrifices involved in achieving your chosen reality, such as devoting some of your leisure time to the project, they hardly seem like sacrifices at all. This is because you are so motivated to achieve your end results that you *want* to do those things that will contribute to that reality, much more than you want to do the things you are "sacrificing."

## Patience and Programming

Although the Mental Movie can help us attain results we formerly thought were impossible, there may be times when it seems as though it didn't work and you have failed. With a strong, positive self-image, such setbacks or delays in your progress will not be a problem. Often you will find that what appeared to be a failure, wasn't that at all.

Here is an example: A man who attended one of my workshops informed me that he was going to program for an improvement in the working conditions of his job. Two days later his wife, who also was in the workshop, phoned me to say that her husband had been fired. I told her that perhaps it was for the best, and that this could free him to take advantage of another opportunity. Three days after our conversation she called again and told me her husband had been offered another job that he considered at least twice as good as the previous one. She added that he would not have been exposed to the new job if he had not lost the old one.

No programming is wasted. It accumulates and builds, even though sometimes it takes a while to see the results in physical reality. Suppose you program to become a better bowler. You visualize and feel yourself bowling as you would like. You have the approach, backswing, release, follow-through, and the ball is rolling just the way you want. You hit the pocket, and all the pins go down. You feel the thrill of the strike and the happiness and satisfaction of accomplishing what you had set out to do. A moment later you pick up your ball and attempt to duplicate in physical reality what you just experienced in your mind. However, something goes awry. Instead of a strike, you get a gutter ball. Does this mean that your programming was a waste of time? Not at all. It merely means that it has not yet manifested itself in your physical reality. *But it will!* This is not to say that eventually you will *always* get strikes, but the programming you have done will eventually influence your performance for the better.

When we plant seeds in a garden we aren't disappointed if the plants don't spring up in "Jack and the Beanstalk" fashion. We are patient. We know that the forces of nature are at work and we will soon have the fruits of our endeavors. We must have the same patience with our mental programming. Emerson said, "Adopt the pace of nature: her secret is patience."

There is often a gap in time between inner and outer reality. It's only a matter of time before our inner reality manifests itself in our outer reality. With some projects we enjoy immediate results, and with others we may have to wait a while.

## Can You Program for More than One Thing at a Time?

Yes, you can program for many things in the same session. After the initial Mental Movie session, you only use the film with the positive end result. This only takes thirty to sixty seconds. Then you release that goal image and you can dwell on another end result, enjoy it for thirty to sixty seconds, and release it and dwell on another end result, and so on. You could program for half a dozen different things in five minutes. It takes less than one minute to relax your mind using the three deep breaths and a minute or less for each project.

Here's an example. One young man in Minneapolis programmed for bowling, golf, weight control, and business all at the same time. Here's what happened:

1. He improved his bowling average from 180 to 195, although he bowled only in his league one night a week. He did not practice physically—only mentally. He also bowled a 300 game and a 700 series.

2. He programmed to win at least one golf tournament during the next year. He won *four* golf tournaments.

3. He wanted to take off fifty pounds in a short time. Three months later he was fifty pounds lighter and never felt better. The last time I saw him, which was several years later, he had taken off another ten pounds.

4. He programmed to improve his creativity and income and to own an architectural firm within four years. In only two years he owned an architectural firm and was sending all of his employees to my workshop. He was also successful with several other projects. With all this success, he still says he has just begun. He realizes that he has just scratched the surface of his potential, and he expects to get better and better.

Another example of someone programming for more than one thing at a time is revealed in a note from a successful businessman who had attended my workshop. He informed me that in the seven months since completing the workshop he had:

1. Quit smoking.

2. Quit drinking alcohol.

3. Lost fifty pounds—now at his football-playing weight of seventeen years ago.

4. Quit drinking caffeine—only drinks herb teas.

5. Started jogging—now at four miles, seven days per week, in thirty-five minutes.

6. Went from size fifty-four suit to forty-eight, and size forty-six waist to forty-one.

He further reported the goals that he had written had all been met; he was making more money than ever, and was writing new goals already.

I could fill a book with true stories of positive end results people have related to me after programming themselves for prosperity. Even those who begin as skeptics are rewarded by applying their minds in this way. A successful businessman who was skeptical about the power of programming asked me if I thought it would work in helping him collect twenty-five thousand dollars that another businessman had owed to him for over two years. He said he had little or no hope of ever collecting this money. I told him to use the Mental Movie technique at least three times a day, and each time to picture himself meeting with this man and receiving the money.

A few days later he informed me that the man who owed him the money telephoned to arrange a meeting at O'Hare Airport in Chicago because he wanted to pay his debt. They met, the debt was paid, and the skeptic became a believer.

## VISUALIZATION FOR WINNING CONTESTS

Many people have improved their financial condition by programming to win contests. One of them is Helen Hadsell, who has been written up in national magazines as the woman who wins every contest she enters. She has won hundreds of contests and has received prizes such as trips to resorts all over the United States, trips to Europe, automobiles, furniture for her home, scholarships for her children, a home that is worth about $150,000, and on and on.

Helen describes her success in a book she wrote called *The Name It and Claim It Game.* She also does workshops. I invited her to do workshops in Minneapolis a couple of times to share her techniques. Wherever she goes she inspires people to enter contests and become winners. Although I think that there are much better things to do with your money than buy lottery tickets, I know of two people in Illinois, each of whom won the big jackpot in the Illinois lottery, and another who won fifty thousand dollars by applying the ideas that Helen advocates, which is basically directing energy, similar to the Mental Movie technique. When Helen programs to win a prize, in her mind, that prize is hers. She has already won it. She owns it. She is enjoying it. She creates an inner reality that manifests itself at the physical dimension. If it's a new car, she's driving that car. She owns it; it's hers. If it's a stove, she's cooking on that stove. As soon as she enters that contest, in her mind she has won. To illustrate how confident she is in winning, as soon as she entered the contest for the new house, she immediately went out and bought a lot for the house.

Helen is very intuitive, and weeks after the contest had closed, they still hadn't heard anything from the sponsoring company, but she woke up one morning and told her husband, "Today they are going to call us to tell us that we won the house." Her husband said, "Okay, I'll make sure I'm home to take the call." She told her children that when they got home from school the contest people would be there, and that whatever they do they should act surprised. When the children came home from school, the contest people were there. Incidentally, they were surprised that Helen had already bought a lot for the house. I know quite a few people who decided that if Helen could do it, maybe they could do it, too.

Many of the people in my classes have won valuable prizes such as trips to Europe and automobiles. Here's a note that was on a Christmas card I received.

> Thank you for your invitation to drop by for your open house. I will be delighted.
>
> I was a grand prize sweepstake winner and won ten thousand dollars, and a Chevy Caprice Coupe (know of anyone who would like to buy it?), a mink coat, a home Panasonic video system, which includes a nineteen-inch color TV set, remote control, a recorder, and a color camera, a vacation for two to Hawaii, and a vacation for two to the Caribbean. Sounds like fiction, doesn't it? I have most of the prizes, but still have to hear from the travel companies.
>
> I am also completing a book, which will be published this summer, so things are looking up for me, especially since my MS is in total remission. See you next week.
>
> Loretta Girzaitis

I personally haven't been motivated to enter contests, although I recently won a trip to Paris, but it may be something you'll decide to do and do successfully. Someone has to win; why not you? You might wonder what happens if many people are programming to win the same prize. If that should happen, the prize would go to the person who has the greatest need, desire, belief, and expectancy. It also depends on how often the person programs. If you program three times a day, every day, you are more likely to be successful than the person who only programs once a day. The more we practice, the more we develop the power of our mind.

One afternoon in a meeting at my office with a salesman and a contractor, both of whom had been students of mine and who program regularly, the salesman began to tell us about a banquet he had recently attended. He said that he decided he would win the big door prize. It was something he wanted and needed, and he proceeded to tell everyone that he was going to win it. They laughed at him and said he was crazy, but he insisted he was the winner. When the time came to announce the prize winner, he got up from his chair and was more than halfway to the stage when they called his name. He had won!

But that's only part of the story, because while it was being told, the contractor had a big grin on his face and kept saying, "Yes, yes, that's the way it happened." He finally explained that the exact thing had just happened to him. He told everyone he was the winner, they laughed, and he was halfway to the stage when his name was called. Different banquet, different prize, but same kind of belief and expectancy.

Although the Mental Movie is a priceless tool for attracting money, using more of your potential, and achieving success in any area of life, it won't help you unless you use it, and a good time to start is right now.

1. Think of how you would like to improve any area of your life.

2. Relax your mind by closing your eyes and taking three deep breaths, holding each for five to ten seconds, and while exhaling say, "Relax."

3. Run the first reel of the Mental Movie (the current situation) for a few minutes.

4. Run the reel of the end results you desire for thirty to sixty seconds. Feel the energy and positive emotions.

**5.** Release it and relax, knowing that you have received immediate benefits, and the best is yet to come.

**6.** Rerun the positive reel often, preferably three times a day.

The Mental Movie will bring better and better results as you continue to use it. After using it many times, you may discover you can relax your mind completely with one deep breath and use the technique with your eyes open. You will be able to use it while walking, exercising, and doing things that require little mental effort such as mowing the lawn, shoveling snow, ironing, vacuuming, bathing, shaving, or attending a yodeling concert.

I often use the Mental Movie in situations that used to try my patience, such as standing in line at theaters, restaurants, and stores, or waiting at bus stops, red lights, and railroad crossings. It can also be used while waiting for someone who is late for an appointment. I used to consider most of the above situations as a waste of time, and often this attitude caused me to feel very negative and irritable. Now these situations are viewed as opportunities to program for myself, for others, and for the world. There is no wasted time when you apply the Mental Movie.

This technique, along with your affirmations, will hasten your progress outward on your spiral to greater success, health, and happiness. And you will find the remaining chapters on self-image, goals, and valuable tips for successful living will further assure your total success.

# CHAPTER 4

# BUILDING A HEALTHY, PROSPEROUS SELF-IMAGE

*It is only when the person decides, "I am someone; I am someone worth being; I am committed to being myself," that change becomes possible.*

Carl R. Rogers

# Your Best Friend or
# Your Worst Enemy?

In your quest for success, financial and otherwise, your self-image can be your best friend or your worst enemy. A positive self-image can guide you to prosperity and a totally successful life, whereas a negative self-image can destroy your business and personal relationships, make it difficult to learn, rob you of your health, and prevent you from developing your potential and from experiencing success in all areas of life.

What is self-image and why is it so powerful? Self-image is the mental picture we have of ourselves as being a certain kind of person. We may not realize that we have a mental picture or inner image of ourselves, but we all do. And we will do nothing that is inconsistent with this inner image—self-image—even though it is not necessarily based on truth. Self-image is based on what we think of ourselves—what we *believe* to be true.

Psychologists state that the self-image is the core of our personality. Every aspect of human behavior is affected by the self-image: the ability to learn; the capacity to grow and change; the choice of friends, mates, and careers. Psychologists claim that a strong, positive self-image is the best possible assurance of success in life.

Technically, it is possible to have a good self-image in certain areas of life but not much self-esteem (self-acceptance or self-love). For example, you could see yourself as being good-looking, an outstanding scholar, a great athlete, or a successful businessperson, and still not like yourself. However, a person's *total self-image* is not going to be positive if self-esteem is lacking. Therefore, in this book, when a positive self-image is mentioned, it is assumed that high self-esteem is included.

## YOUR SELF-IMAGE DETERMINES YOUR FEELINGS AND BEHAVIOR

How you feel right now depends on your self-image. How happy you are, how successful, how healthy, how intelligent, how confident, how loving, and how lovable all depend on your self-image. What kind of day or week you had was determined by your self-image. How well you get along with other people, how well you perform in school or at home or at work, how it is going to be for you tomorrow and all of next week and for the rest of your life will depend on your self-image.

Your self-image controls everything you feel and do. It is vitally important. How you give and receive love is determined by the mental pictures of yourself. Your ability to experience this book and make its techniques part of your everyday existence begins with your self-image.

# You Can Change Your Self-Image

You'll recall that in chapter 1 I mentioned that many years ago I developed a self-image and goal achievement workshop that later was included in a more comprehensive personal development program called Productive Meditation®. In those early workshop years, Dr. Nancy Crewe, a counseling psychologist at the University of Minnesota, administered the Tennessee Self-Concept Scale, which included pre- and post-testing, to the workshop participants to determine the effect the workshops had on an individual self-concept.

The post-testing occurred weeks after the presentation of the workshop. Her conclusions were: "The inventory scores show that participants felt better about basic identity, their behavior, their bodies, themselves as members of families, and communities—every aspect of identity which was measured—after taking the workshop. These scores are particularly impressive in view of the fact that there was no change in their scores on the self-criticism scale (this indicates that they were equally frank and open to normal, healthy, self-criticism on both tests)."

Additional research by Dr. Crewe included the use of Rotter's Scale (a highly regarded instrument for measuring personality adjustment) to measure internal versus external control. This research revealed that after the workshop, participants were feeling more in control of their lives and described themselves as more active, striving, achieving, powerful, independent, and effective.

This research definitely established that the self-image can be significantly improved in a short period of time. This is important because when we improve our self-image, we automatically improve our lives.

## Improve Your Self-Image with Mental Programming

An excellent way to improve your self-image is to mentally program yourself with positive thoughts, images, and feelings. This can be done through the use of the Mental Movie explained in chapter 3. The affirmations given in chapter 2 and at the end of this chapter are also useful tools for improving self-image.

Dr. Maxwell Maltz explained the use of mental programming in his book *Psycho-Cybernetics*. He compared the brain and the nervous system to a computer. Of course, we are not machines or computers, but our brain functions like a computer. Our brain and nervous system or computer, if you want to call it that, cannot tell the difference between something we vividly *imagine* and something we *actually experience*. So if we use our imagination properly, it will have the same impact on our lives as if we had actually experienced and performed what we imagined.

In *Psycho-Cybernetics*, Dr. Maltz tells how mental practice improved the shooting skills of basketball players. Seventy-five basketball players were divided into three groups of twenty-five each. The first group was told to practice shooting free throws for twenty minutes a day for twenty days. The second group was told to ignore basketball for twenty days—no thinking about it, no touching the basketball. The third group was told not to touch a basketball for the twenty-day period, but for twenty minutes a day to vividly imagine themselves shooting free throws and doing it perfectly. If they missed a shot in their imagination, they were to correct their aim accordingly.

At the end of the twenty-day period, the group that practiced physically showed a 24 percent improvement; the group that did not touch a basketball and did not think about basketball showed no improvement; and the group that did not physically touch a basketball but used their imagination to shoot free throws showed a 23 percent improvement—almost the same improvement as those who practiced physically. If this last group had practiced both mentally and physically, their improvement would have been even greater.

Golfers such as Ben Hogan and Jack Nicklaus have used mental techniques, also. Hogan called it a muscle memory. When he was mentally practicing, he imagined his brain was sending signals to his muscles, and later when he went to swing the club, his muscles remembered how to accomplish the swing. Jack Nicklaus uses a mental movie. He says that he envisions each shot in his mind just the way he wants it to be—back swing, follow-through, the flight of the ball, where it is going to wind up—at least five times before he even selects his club. Roberto Clemente, a member of baseball's Hall of Fame, used to sit in the locker room before a game, calm his mind, and then imagine himself batting against the opposing team's pitcher for that game. In his mind he would hit the ball perfectly each time. When he walked out on the field, he was confident, a winner in his own mind and on the field.

Steve Braun, batting instructor with the Boston Red Sox, has taught programming techniques to many major league hitters with great success. In fact, he frequently uses my tapes, particularly the one entitled *Peak Performance in Sports*.

Some years ago a high school swimming coach

asked me to teach his swimmers how to use their minds to improve their swimming performance. I did, giving the coach some tips on follow-up and reinforcement. In their next meet they broke several school records. (Unfortunately, my son Bob was a member of the opposing team, but later that season Bob broke a team record for the five-hundred-meter freestyle, and the following year set a few more records. He had also learned mental programming.)

Coaches and athletes, like Olympic stars who win the gold medal in their minds before actually winning on the field, have become aware of the tremendous importance of mental practice or programming. But this is not limited to sports.

Everything we do involves our minds, so mental programming can be used to improve any area of our lives—anything we choose to do. You can use the mind to generally improve your self-concept, or to improve your business, sales, personal relationships, health, learning, and so forth. You can mentally program yourself for success.

In the computer industry there is a saying, "GIGO"—garbage in, garbage out. You can have a multimillion-dollar computer, but if you only program it with nonsense, that is all it will be good for. So often we find that in the past we have allowed our mental computer to be programmed with limitations, fears, and other garbage. We can receive this kind of programming from friends, relatives, teachers, television, movies, and a variety of other sources, including ourselves. All this negative programming, or garbage, prevents us from using our mind's potential.

Some say that we only use 10 percent of our mind; Einstein said we only use 5 percent; Margaret Mead said 4 percent; and some scientists say 1 percent or less. What if we could double or triple that percentage? What would our lives be like? What would the world be like? What would life be like if everyone was thinking more creatively and functioning more effectively? Mental programming can help us increase this percentage.

## RELEASE THE GENIUS WITHIN YOU

Buckminster Fuller, a dear friend and member of the board of advisors of Effective Learning Systems, Inc., before his death said, "Every child is born a genius, but is enslaved by the misconceptions and self-doubt of the adult world and spends much of his/her life having to unlearn that perspective." Because I believe that is true, I have dedicated my career to helping people free themselves from the misconceptions and self-doubt that entrap them. This book can show people not only how to attract money but how to discover and develop their potential—how to be what they were meant, and want, to be. To do this, it is necessary to eliminate self-imposed mental limitations.

Animals show us how easy it is to acquire self-imposed mental limitations. Fleas, elephants, and northern pike are good examples.

Fleas are interesting little fellows. They bite and they are great jumpers. They can jump higher perhaps than any other creatures for their size.

If we put a flea in a container, the flea will jump above the rim of that container. After a while we put a lid on the container and observe what happens. The flea continues to jump but this time hits its head and comes down with a flea-size headache. The flea jumps again, and the same thing happens. This goes on for some time, and then we remove the lid. When we do, we observe the flea. The flea still jumps, but never any higher than where the lid was located. Even though the physical limitation has been removed, the flea thinks it's still there. In a similar experiment, grasshoppers will develop the same limitation.

Elephants also can be controlled through mental limitations. When elephants are not performing in the circus, they are tied up. The little baby elephants are tied with great big ropes to stakes in the ground, and the full-grown elephants are tied with little tiny ropes to stakes in the ground. This really looks dumb because the powerful grown elephants could easily pull out the stakes, but they do not. The reason for this is that when they were younger, they pulled and tugged on the big ropes that were used to tie them and tried to get away. Then one day they gave up and quit pulling. From then on they would just walk to the end of the rope and stop. They had learned their limitations.

Dr. Eden Ryle has produced a training film dealing with self-imposed limitations. The title is *You can Surpass Yourself*. In this film, a northern pike was placed in a big tank of water. Some minnows, the pike's favorite food, were thrown in the water to illustrate how the pike enjoy minnows. The pike ate the minnows quickly. Later, when the pike was hungry again, some more minnows were put in the tank. However, this time they were encased in and protected by a glass tube. The pike tried to get the minnows, but kept bouncing off that glass wall. After a time the pike ignored the minnows in the tube and acted as if the minnows were no longer there. The tube was then removed, and the minnows were set free in the water with the pike. Do you know what happened? The pike starved to death. His favorite food was all around him, and still he starved to death.

Of course, we are not northern pike, and we are not elephants; nor are we fleas or grasshoppers. However, we can learn from these experiments because we have all accepted limitations. We have said, "I can't do this," and "I can't do that," and it became our reality. The mental limitation became as real as a physical limitation, and just as formidable. How much more of what we call reality isn't reality, but only our acceptance of it? As we demonstrated in chapter 2, we have created realities for ourselves that are limited; or, as Richard Bach might say, "We have created our illusions."

## ONE WOMAN'S EVALUATION OF HOW SHE CHANGED HER SELF-IMAGE

About two years after attending my workshop, a young woman named Betty sent me a letter that included the following list of dramatic changes she had already experienced as a result of applying the techniques she had learned in the workshop.

| BEFORE | AFTER |
|---|---|
| Height: 5'2" Weight: 152 lbs. | Height: 5'2" Weight: 118 lbs. |
| Depressed with life. | Impressed with life. |
| Shy, uninvolved, uncaring. | Sharing, concerned, loving. |
| Felt insignificant, and didn't look at a person ever when speaking to them. I stared at the floor and shuffled my feet. | Self-assured, reaching out to others to share our ideas. Made eye contact and felt open with gestures and expressions. |

Slouching with a feeling of "what's the use." I had nothing to look forward to.

Standing tall with the knowledge that I'm okay, and getting better and better every day.

Trapped in an unhappy relationship, not knowing how to escape, to get by on my own.

Free and happy to be able to live independently, and fully realize the person I am.

Surviving on old programming. Being manipulated by what I was told to do or feel. Accepting guilty feelings and slavery tasks as what I was put here for.

Living a real life. No longer a robot in motion, but a real living person striving for goals and reaching them. I'm here to make life better ...for me and those around me.

My speech was difficult to understand. I stuttered and looked away from the receiver, feeling I wasn't good enough to talk to them.

I speak to people as their equal, able to show expression with confidence. The more I openly communicate, the better I feel.

My children were insecure due to my constant, depressed state of mind.

My children are secure with the feeling of having a happy, confident, dependable mother.

I found no joy in being a mother, no rewards in it, just an obligation.

Delighted to be an important part in the lives of these beautiful individuals.

Paranoid, certain that every person who knew me plotted against me. Tried to please everyone, and ended up by not knowing who was the real me. I was thought of as unreliable and inconsistent.

Self-fulfilled, pleased with myself. Able to accept the fact that not everyone will like me; but I am perfectly me and proud of it. I am respected for not being wishy-washy.

Learning problems. High school dropout.

Presently attending college. Maintaining B+ average, with current career in business data entry.

# BECOME YOUR OWN BEST FRIEND

A very important step in building a healthy, positive self-image is to become your own best friend. Many people are their own worst enemy. As Pogo says, "We have met the enemy, and he is us." With a greater awareness, this no longer will be true.

Why would you want to be your own best friend? What does that mean? Does it mean you will be narcissistic? That you will love only yourself? Be self-centered? Be conceited?

Not at all! To be your own best friend is to accept yourself unconditionally, just as you would any dear friend. It means to be honest, supportive, warm, and loving. We are all supposed to be created in the image of God, and as the saying goes, "God doesn't make junk." When we put ourselves down, we are putting down our Creator, and we are short-circuiting the love energy that is available to us. Og Mandino points out in his book, *The Greatest Miracle in the World*, that great works of art are valuable for two reasons: They are created by masters and are few in number. Therefore, you are an extremely valuable treasure because there is only one of you, and you were created by the greatest Master of all.

Becoming a good friend to yourself makes it easier for you to be a good friend to others, and easier for them to be a good friend to you. The more we recognize our own worth and value, the more we can recognize the worth and value of others and the more we can discover, develop, and use our potential to help others, our family and friends, and the world. We are then moving outward on our spiral toward unlimited reality, toward greater prosperity and happiness.

# Who Is the Real You?

Let's take time to become even better acquainted with the *real* you. Take a good look at yourself. You are a trinity of mind, body, and spirit. You are a *unique* human being. Considering all the possibilities in the process of your conception, any one of 300 billion humans could have been born, each different from the other. But it was you who started a new life. It was no accident. You have a reason for being here. You occupy a special place in this world, and you are becoming more aware of the good within you and your potential for greatness.

Within you there is power—a good and constructive kind of power. As a result, the most powerful things you will ever experience are within you. Your thoughts and actions can and do literally change the lives of those around you. You can make each day a little better (and often much better) for every person you meet. Think about that! Think of the effect you can have on human lives through the use of a smile, a thought, a pleasant tone of voice, a sincere compliment. This is power—and it is a wonderful, constructive use of power.

## Are You a Positive or Negative Influence?

You are already a powerful influence on this planet. As insignificant as you may feel at times, let me assure you that your being here has made a difference. You have touched the lives of many people. Your influence can be positive or negative. The choice is yours.

For example, let's say you go to work or school one day and before you arrive, you experience some kind of irritation or inconvenience, such as someone cutting in front of you in traffic or being delayed by a train. When you arrive at your destination, you may take out your frustration on one or more people by being negative, overly critical, and unpleasant in a variety of ways.

Do you think that your negativity will be absorbed by the individuals to whom you direct it and stop there? Not likely. They will pass that negativity on to others (perhaps many others), and each of those people will pass it on to others, and each of them in turn to others. You have started a chain reaction that can reach hundreds, and in some cases thousands, of people and influence them in a *negative* way—people you have never even seen. Often the negativity will work its way back to you. And even when it does not, you pay a heavy price because you keep the original of whatever you project. You just send a copy.

Now let's look at the flip side. Suppose you experience the same event in traffic but choose not to let it influence you in a negative way. When you arrive at work, you are more likely to be friendly and supportive and give people sincere compliments (a compliment should always be sincere, even when you do not mean it). Each of these people will pass on your positive influence to others, and each of them will pass it on to others, and you have started a chain reaction that can reach hundreds, and in some cases thousands, of people in a *positive* way. Once again you keep the original and just send out a copy. In addition, the positives in the positive chain reactions have a way of coming back to you, so you are likely to receive additional benefits, even if you do not expect them.

You have *already* been doing this. You have been influencing a great number of people, sometimes positively, sometimes negatively, with perhaps little or no effort or awareness of the consequences. Now with greater awareness you may choose to be more of a positive influence on others, and you can multiply the power of this influence by projecting loving energy.

## Programming for Positivity

Everything we think, see, hear, or experience can be considered programming for our mental computer. Constantly "seeds" are being planted in our "garden." Try the following programming exercise.

Begin any programming exercise by calming your mind. You can do this by taking three deep breaths, holding each one a few seconds, and while exhaling slowly, saying to yourself, "Relax." This mind calming can be used with or without closing your eyes. Since you need to read this particular exercise, keep your eyes open. As soon as you are mentally relaxed (carefree), tell yourself that as you read the following words, you are going to mentally "hear" a pleasant, strong, loving, soothing voice talking to you with great sincerity and care for your growth and development. Are you ready? Read.

You are now developing a healthy appreciation of yourself. You recognize and appreciate the good within you so it will materialize; it will continue to develop, making your life more meaningful, more important. It will touch the lives of other people; it will help to make this world a better place in which to live. You are becoming happier every day that you are who you are and that no one else can fill your place in this world or be exactly like you.

You are beginning to notice the positive things

about yourself and cancel the negative thoughts, although you recognize you are not perfect and perhaps never will be; but you are improving every day. You will make mistakes (everyone does), but you will learn from them, and you will search for something good in every temporary failure, defeat, or adversity you experience. You will recognize and benefit from the lessons, insights, and opportunities that come with all unpleasant things one experiences.

You are beginning to make every experience, whether it is pleasant or unpleasant, yield some form of benefit. You will balance your life, leading to peace of mind. Above all, you are developing a good feeling about yourself. Every day you are feeling more and more comfortable with yourself, and you are becoming your own best friend. It is a beautiful feeling to really like yourself and enjoy being you. As this feeling develops, you find it quite natural to direct the same feelings toward others, and you begin to appreciate, like, and enjoy them more and more.

Every day you are becoming more aware of your assets and the qualities and beauty within you. You are discovering more of your potential every day and using it to help yourself and others. Deep inside you are a lovable child, every bit as lovable as any little baby. You love that little child within and encourage it to grow, evolve, and develop. You are becoming your own best friend. When you are a good friend to yourself, it is easier to be a good friend to others, and easier for them to be a good friend to you. You are nourishing yourself with good and positive thoughts, images, and feelings. (Feel the love.) You are surrounding yourself with people who nourish you.

You forgive yourself and others. You radiate love wherever you go. (Feel the love.)

Take a moment to enjoy the feeling of liking yourself and being happy you are who you are. Mentally say, "Thank you," and as you do, allow yourself to *feel* the thanks.

You may experience a tingling sensation as you repeat mentally "thank you" or a feeling of well-being or satisfaction similar to the way you have felt in the past when you were very pleased or happy. Allow yourself to experience any pleasant feeling as you say "thank you" for whatever you may have to be thankful for—for just being you.

Now slowly let the voice you "heard" fade away. The positive words you just read will make your life more rewarding today. You will find it helpful to reread the above passage once a day for twenty-one days. This programming exercise is part of the script for my *Self-Image Programming* audiocassette tape. I will be happy to send it to you as a gift along with a free catalog of hundreds of tapes and other self-help products. Please enclose $3.00 for shipping and handling. See page 177 for details.

Mentally saying "thank you" releases the positive recordings we have stored in our brain. These words trigger a reliving of the positive emotions that go along with such a recording. I discovered this by accident when I was programming many years ago. I was enjoying a relaxed state of mind and body and suddenly the words *thank you* came to me. And as they did, I began to feel twice as good, even euphoric, as if something truly wonderful had just happened to me, and I was enjoying and appreciating it thoroughly. Then I wondered if I could use these words as a triggering mechanism to reexperience that feeling whenever I desired. I discovered that I could indeed change my mood and feel euphoric by mentally saying, "Thank you," and allowing myself to *feel* the "thanks." Try it yourself and see what you experience. You will also find it beneficial to say, "I love you," to yourself and allow yourself to *feel* the love.

## LOVE YOUR BODY

Another important step in becoming your own best friend is to occasionally take a few moments to appreciate each part of your body. Recognize the beauty of every part. Know that each part of your body is functioning in a more rhythmic and healthy manner, and no matter what your previous thoughts were, you now begin to recognize that every portion of your body is a beautiful and important part of nature.

Many years ago I had a very negative self-concept about my physical body, and the more I thought of myself that way, the more this became a reality. I was projecting the image of an unattractive person. When you think of yourself as unattractive, other people begin to view you in the same manner. In the past, if someone were to call me "ugly," I would have been thoroughly crushed as I silently agreed. If it were to happen now, I might say, "You should have seen me before," as I silently reaffirm that I am okay in that respect.

Every second, millions of our cells die and are replaced by millions more. Our minds have the blueprint for the reproduction of these new cells. When we think in terms of being unattractive or in poor health, we can influence this reproduction in a negative way. If we are thinking in terms of being healthy and attractive, we can influence this reproduction in a positive way. The results of my change in thinking about my physical body have been very gratifying because my health and appearance have improved tremendously. The more you allow yourself to think that you are attractive, the more attractive you will be in your eyes and in the eyes of others. You will bring out your inner beauty; and believe me, it is there waiting to be released.

## Affirm Your Good Qualities

As you know by now, another helpful tool for programming your mind positively is the use of success statements. The following is a list of success statements regarding self-image. You may want to make copies of this list so you can use it several times.

Read them and score yourself on a scale of one to five (five being the most true about yourself).

---

## I AM:

| | | | |
|---|---|---|---|
| Loving | 1 2 3 4 5 | Talented | 1 2 3 4 5 |
| Lovable | 1 2 3 4 5 | Efficient | 1 2 3 4 5 |
| Intelligent | 1 2 3 4 5 | Prosperous | 1 2 3 4 5 |
| Productive | 1 2 3 4 5 | Assertive | 1 2 3 4 5 |
| Goal Oriented | 1 2 3 4 5 | Tactful | 1 2 3 4 5 |
| Aware | 1 2 3 4 5 | Open-minded | 1 2 3 4 5 |
| Honest | 1 2 3 4 5 | Appreciative | 1 2 3 4 5 |
| Friendly | 1 2 3 4 5 | Ambitious | 1 2 3 4 5 |
| Warm | 1 2 3 4 5 | Courageous | 1 2 3 4 5 |

| | | | |
|---|---|---|---|
| Dynamic | 1 2 3 4 5 | Thoughtful | 1 2 3 4 5 |
| Enthusiastic | 1 2 3 4 5 | Tolerant | 1 2 3 4 5 |
| Persistent | 1 2 3 4 5 | Loyal | 1 2 3 4 5 |
| Witty | 1 2 3 4 5 | Understanding | 1 2 3 4 5 |
| Decisive | 1 2 3 4 5 | Kind | 1 2 3 4 5 |
| Attractive | 1 2 3 4 5 | Energetic | 1 2 3 4 5 |
| Dependable | 1 2 3 4 5 | Fun to Be With | 1 2 3 4 5 |
| Good Listener | 1 2 3 4 5 | Positive | 1 2 3 4 5 |
| Affectionate | 1 2 3 4 5 | Considerate | 1 2 3 4 5 |
| Creative | 1 2 3 4 5 | Healthy | 1 2 3 4 5 |
| Patient | 1 2 3 4 5 | Happy | 1 2 3 4 5 |
| Supportive | 1 2 3 4 5 | Successful | 1 2 3 4 5 |
| Optimistic | 1 2 3 4 5 | Natural | 1 2 3 4 5 |

You have all of the positive qualities listed above, in great abundance, and much more. You may not *always* feel loving, lovable, intelligent, aware, and so on. Few people, if any, do. And it is no wonder we do not, considering all the negative programming to which we have been exposed. Often the humility that we have been taught has been overdone. Free yourself from the bonds of negative programming and program new positive thoughts, images, and feelings that will change your self-image for the better.

Begin by studying your scores. You can improve any low scores. Begin with those that you marked 1, 2, or 3. Insert your name and write each one ten times in the first, second, and third persons. For example: "I, Bob, am prosperous"; "You, Bob, are prosperous"; and "He, Bob, is prosperous." It is helpful to use first, second, and third person because we have received negative programming in all three persons. After using the success statements for three weeks, score yourself again. Then affirm those you have marked four or less for three or more weeks. Since the success statements are short, you can affirm several different statements in one brief affirmation session.

You may reinforce your affirmations by writing some on a card that you carry in your wallet or purse. You can glance at them whenever it is convenient for you throughout the day. Say them to yourself and allow yourself to feel the appropriate emotions. Imagine yourself looking, acting, and feeling each affirmation. Imagine also how other people will act, look, and feel in response. Use your imagination and let it become and feel very real for you. Involve all your senses and really enjoy being the way you choose to be.

Since music activates the right hemisphere of the brain and accelerates the learning process, you may find it helpful to put your affirmations to music. Whenever you hear a song, try to fit the affirmation into the song. Replace the words of the song with your affirmations. This will help you make a deeper impression on your mental computer.

The more we recognize the good qualities in ourselves, the more we will see them in others. The mind cannot focus on both the negative and the positive at the same time. When we are thinking of these positive qualities in ourselves and others, we are not thinking negatively. At that moment we are free of fear, worry, hate, and other negative thoughts. At that moment we are building for the future—we are making positive mental recording that will strengthen our self-image and enrich our lives. You can also use affirmations to help build the self-image of someone you care for.

For example, when my youngest son, Jeff, was a baby, for some reason I had more than a father's usual concern for this child's health. I wanted him to be strong and healthy, so several times a day I would say to him, along with other positive statements, "You are strong," "I love you," and strong he became. He believed he was strong, and created that reality, which is as real today as it was then. It never occurred to me that my saying "You are strong" had such an influence on him until one day while vacationing in Florida, we were driving to visit Busch Gardens, a zoo and amusement park. The whole family was excited about this new experience, and we could hardly wait to see the lions and other animals. As we neared the entrance, three-year-old Jeff, who was sitting in the backseat, stood up, poked his head between my wife and me, and with saucerlike eyes filled with joy and wonder, blurted out, "Busch Gardens is *strong!*" For Jeff "strong" meant not only physical strength but was almost synonymous with everything good.

Because I had been using the word *strong* when expressing and displaying my love for him, "good," "wonderful," "great," and "strong" all belonged together.

As a young man, Jeff is all of the above—and more. When he was little I often said, "When I grow up I want to be like Jeff." The point here is that I believe he benefited from the positive statements. What you say can help shape the lives of others.

Take time each day to appreciate the miracle of your existence, your body, your mind, your life, your spirit, your entire being. You *are* beautiful. Know that you are important to this world and can be a profound positive influence on humanity. Know that your time on this planet will not be wasted but will be put to good use by the development and use of your natural resources, by your appreciation and love for all humanity beginning with yourself. Become your own best friend, and say to yourself many times each day, "I like you, and I love you, and I always will, no matter what; and I am happy to see you improving every day and making your life more meaningful."

The strengthening of your self-image will not only help you rewrite your life script so it is easier for you to attract money, it will help you to maintain your prosperity and enjoy a happier more fulfilling life.

Additional Success Statements:

❑ **The real me is lovable.**

❑ **I now appreciate who I am.**

❑ **I now recognize my good qualities.**

❑ **I feel good about myself.**

❑ **I'm happy being me.**

❑ **I'm enjoying high self-esteem.**

# CHAPTER 5

# How to Set and Achieve Your Goals

*The greatest thing in the world is not so much where we stand, as in what direction we are moving.*

Oliver Wendell Holmes

An excellent way to assure prosperity and make the most of your life is to set goals. Having goals builds enthusiasm and excitement. Goals help us to get in touch with our creativity and energy and direct them in ways that lead us to satisfaction, confidence, fulfillment, and financial independence.

## YOU ARE MORE IMPORTANT THAN YOUR GOAL

Although it is healthy to be moving toward a goal, it is essential not to tie your self-worth to your goal. You are okay, whether or not the goal is attained. Regardless of the outcome of your endeavors, you are a worthy, unique, lovable human being. By keeping this in mind and applying the techniques offered in the previous chapters, you will experience less negative stress, have more fun, and enjoy greater success.

Most of the very successful people I know have occasionally fallen short of their goals. But instead of letting that "failure" destroy their self-worth, they viewed it as a learning experience and continued on to eventually enjoy even greater success than if they had attained their original goals. Always remember that goals are great tools we can use to achieve our chosen success, but they are never more important than your self-worth.

## GOALS ARE NATURAL, KEEP US YOUNG, AND ALLOW FOR FLEXIBILITY

It is natural to set goals. We are goal-striving mechanisms. We are built to solve problems. When we were very young, we saw other people walking, talking, reading, riding bicycles, and so forth, and we made up our minds that we too would do these things. Without realizing it, we set goals for ourselves. It wasn't always easy to attain these goals, but we kept striving for success. We enjoyed the challenges, the learning processes, and the thrill of accomplishment. This is how we learned to walk and talk and do many other things that now seem so natural and easy for us.

Goals can even help us stay younger and healthier. One of our saddest national statistics is that men, on the average, die two years after retiring. When we work at something for so many years, it becomes a major part of our life, and then when it is suddenly taken away, we may feel as though we have lost the major reason for living, or our will to live. Consequently, our resistance to illness is lower, and we are less capable of surviving.

This perhaps explains why so many creative, goal-oriented people live long, productive lives. We don't retire a president of the United States at age sixty-two or age sixty-five, or an Einstein, or a Schweitzer, or a Mother Teresa, or a Picasso, or a Fuller, or an Edison, or a Margaret Mead. These people did much of their best work after age sixty-five. Grandma Moses didn't even start painting until she was a senior citizen. Comedians George Burns, Jack Benny, Bob Hope, Groucho Marx, Red Skelton, Ed Wynne, Lucille Ball, and Henny Youngman were and are often funnier after sixty-five than before. Looking for the humor in life and sharing it with others helped them stay young, active, and productive.

In most of my workshops, I have people in their sixties, seventies, or eighties who are excited about their futures and are setting long-range goals. They know that their minds can keep them young, healthy, active, and productive. And they realize that the key to all of this is love and a sense of direction or purpose.

At the end of a seminar I conducted for 150 nuns at the Saint Paul Priory, one of the nuns told me, "I am ninety-six years of age, and I agree with everything you said. In fact, I have been living what you are teaching." And it showed. She looked about forty years younger. She set goals and sent love to others in her thoughts and prayers and accepted love for herself. She knew that without love for herself she would have little to give. She has lived a long life because she believes she has some worthwhile things to do.

Any doctor will tell you the will to live is vitally important. Did you know that the death rate for a widow or widower the year after losing a partner is much higher than the death rate for other people the same age? According to Dr. Paul Rosch, director of the American Institute of Stress in Yonkers, New York, quoted in *Time*, June 6, 1983, "Widows die at rates three to thirteen times as high as married women for every major known cause of death." It may be that the other person is our major reason for living. And when that person dies, our will to live dies also.

Think about bicycle riding. While moving forward it is easy to keep your balance, but it is very difficult, if not impossible, to do so while staying in one place. Goals help keep us young and healthy. This is particularly true if we are in love with life and determined to make good use of it.

*There is no lack of flexibility with goals.* You can change your goals anytime you desire. It only takes about ten minutes to write a new one. In fact, you have *less* freedom if you have no goals. When you have not set a course, you can be blown around by the winds (and by other people) at whim. Without goals you lose control. Without goals you are not really in charge of your life.

## Make a List of Your Desires

The first step in determining your goals is to make a list of everything you would like to be, gain, possess, or accomplish in any area of life. There are *no limitations*. It doesn't matter if you are too old or too young, do not have enough money or enough education. Disregard all limitations for the moment and just write anything that comes to mind. These are not goals. You are not committed to doing these things. You are merely clarifying many of your desires. However, with prosperity consciousness most, if not all, of your desires become more easily attainable.

The following examples of desires were written by people who have attended my workshops. You may include these on your list:

1. Obtain a college degree.

2. Take off one hundred pounds.

3. Learn about a foreign country

4. Visit Europe.

5. Have a happy marriage.

6. Become a supervisor, foreman, manager, or president of my company.

7. Climb Mount Everest.

8. Own a yacht.

9. Write a book.

10. Have my poetry published.

11. Own a Lear jet and pop-up toaster.

12. Raise bowling average twenty points.

13. Play piano well.

14. Do important work in civic, fraternal, or religious organization.

15. Quit smoking.

16. Help my children through college.

17. Become financially independent.

18. Speak several languages fluently.

19. Go around the world.

20. Own my own business.

21. Learn to hang glide.

22. Swim the English Channel.

23. Write a song.

24. Become famous.

25. Kick a habit.

26. Improve golf score by ten strokes.

27. Donate large amounts of money to my favorite charities.

28. Quit drinking.

29. Be a good painter.

30. Be able to help my friends and family financially.

Make a list of everything you would like to be, gain, possess, or accomplish in any area of life. Use the space on page 102 or a separate sheet of paper.

This list can be quite long. Some people have written one hundred or more items for their lists. Remember these are not goals, but they can give you ideas for goals, and we will use them later.

## Turn Work into Fun

Richard Bach often gives this advice: "Find what you love most, and do it." And if you encounter a delay in doing what you love, find something you love about what you are already doing. Work ought to be fun, and you *can* turn work into fun merely by choosing to make it so and looking for fun in whatever you are doing. The fun is there, just waiting for you to discover it.

You may not choose to continue in your present occupation for the rest of your life, but you will derive many benefits by finding enjoyment in it, until you move on to something even better. Abundance flows into your life when you love what you are doing.

Here are a few of the benefits of finding the fun in what you are doing, and loving it:

- The time you spend working goes much faster.
- You'll have more energy at the end of the day.
- Your relationships, both on the job and off, improve.
- You experience less negative stress.
- You are more productive.
- It helps open the door to what is really important to you—and you are better prepared to do it well and joyfully.

I have had jobs that I have initially hated. Then I decided to make the most of them; and as a result, these jobs not only became more enjoyable, but they turned out to be great learning experiences. They were stepping-stones to greater success and enjoyment.

Another way to get started doing the things you love is to make the following three lists:

**1.** Ten things I love to do.

**2.** Ten ways I can earn money doing these things to benefit others.

**3.** Ten ways I can do these things for large numbers of people, profitably.

Take a few moments right now to write these three lists.

Writing these lists has helped many people see opportunities to do things they love, profitably, and have the confidence to get on with it. I recently received a letter from a man who was going through a divorce when he attended my Productive Meditation® workshop. He said that in the two years since he learned goal setting from me he had:

- Survived the divorce with high self-esteem.
- Controlled his excessive drinking.
- Taken off thirty pounds of excess weight—and kept it off.
- Achieved his goal to have his own business within five years (in less than two years).
- Raised his yearly income from twenty-two thousand to over one hundred thousand dollars.
- Purchased the Corvette he dreamed of owning, and expects to have a Ferrari soon.

He ended his letter by urging me to tell my students to keep programming, because their goals are out there for the asking.

# Use the "Great Eight" to Succeed with Your Goals

*Eight Great Things to Do to Help
You Achieve Your Goals*

1. Write them down.
2. Be specific.
3. Make sure they are *your* goals.
4. Share your goals only with people who will react positively.
5. Use pictures or symbols.
6. Make a commitment.
7. Persist.
8. Program for your goals at least three times a day.

**1.** *Write them down.* This is the most important step in goal setting. Writing your goals is the first step in making your goals physically real. According to various studies, people who write their goals are ten times more likely to achieve their goals than those who have clear goals but don't write them. Writing your goals will also help you crystallize your thinking and help you stay on course. It's a good idea to carry a list of your goals around with you so you can refer to them a few times each day. Writing them will help you be more aware of those goals and more aware of opportunities to help you achieve those goals. You will do things in your daily life that will be consistent with the achievement of those goals, and you will be less likely to do things that are counterproductive. Your written goals also serve as a measurement of your progress. The success you will achieve will come very naturally and will be very con-

sistent with your new beliefs and reality. In fact, some
people hardly notice what great strides they have made
until, sometime after achieving their goals, they come
across the written goals and say, "Wow, I really have
come a long way!"

2. *Be specific.* The more specific you are in writing your goals, the more likely you are to attain them. "I
want more money" is not a goal. That is a wish, but not
a goal. Be specific. How much money? And in what
period of time? Likewise, "I want a better job" is not a
goal. It is a wish, but not a goal. Be specific. What kind
of job do you want? When do you want it?

3. *Make sure they are your goals.* I know people
who are doctors, lawyers, or have other positions seen as
successful, but they don't feel successful because they
are not doing what they really want to do. They wish
they had done something else with their lives. Instead,
they satisfied their parents or another person. It is *your*
life, so make sure they are *your* goals. Do your goals
reflect your values and desires? Are they consistent with
what you love?

4. *Share your goals only with people who will
react positively.* This does not mean you have to ignore
anyone who offers constructive criticism. That can be
helpful at times. But you do want to avoid people who
are habitually negative. People who cannot see how you
can do something if you've never done it before or if
they've never done it can make you doubt yourself. You
may even withdraw from a project that you could have
completed successfully. Surround yourself with positive,
supportive people. Their belief in you will help you to
believe in yourself. They will help you to realize your
potential.

5. *Use pictures or symbols.* You will find it very
helpful to cut out pictures or symbols that will remind

you of your goals and put them in your wallet or purse or on your mirror. Several years ago I met a woman who was in sales and who had some knowledge of goal setting. One of her goals was to own a very expensive foreign sports car. She wanted to purchase that car with cash within five or six months. At her present rate of income, she had no chance of doing that, but she knew something about goal setting, and in addition to writing her goal, she cut out a picture from a brochure of the exact automobile she wanted to own. There was a model standing next to the car, so she took one of her own photographs and cut the head off that photograph and pasted it on top of the model's head.

Every time she saw that picture, she saw herself standing next to the car. She put this picture in her sales book, which she opened frequently each day, to serve as a reminder of her goal. Later she showed that picture to me and said, "That's my car." Then she turned the page, and there was an almost identical picture—same car, same color—but this time it really was a picture of her standing next to the car, and she said, "That's my car." And it was! She had purchased that car five months after setting her goal, and she paid cash for it. She was convinced it would not have happened if she had not used that picture. Looking at it each day and thinking positively inspired her to be more enthusiastic, to make more sales calls, and to be more creative in serving her customers. And her income rose accordingly. Incidentally, the model in the original picture was quite thin and our goal setter managed to take off ten pounds without even trying, which further illustrates the power of mental imagery.

**6.** *Make a commitment.* Something kind of magical happens when you make a commitment to your goals. The moment you definitely commit yourself something steps in to help you—God, the universe, nature. *Help is there.* By committing yourself, you invite that help and increase your energy and ability to succeed. The decision itself sets off a chain reaction of events that assist you and lead you to success. The people, opportunities, and material assistance seem to miraculously appear to support your efforts. As Goethe said:

> Whatever you can do, or dream you can, begin it.
> Boldness has genius, power, and magic in it.

That boldness, power, and magic are waiting to serve you. All you have to do is make a commitment and begin.

The following success statements will help you with your commitment.[1]

- ☐ **I now make a strong commitment to get what I really want.**
- ☐ **Total commitment gives me greater energy.**
- ☐ **When I make a commitment I feel confident and strong.**
- ☐ **I love the feeling of total commitment.**
- ☐ **Commitment makes any goal easier to attain.**

7. *Persist.* Actually, persistence will come automatically if you make a truly firm commitment, but a few words about it here may make it easier for you to

---

[1]Taken from the tape *Commitment and Persistence* ©1990 by Robert E. Griswold. Published by Effective Learning Systems, Inc., Edina, Minnesota.

stay with your commitment. Persistence is a great quality that we all possess. We were born with it. When we were little children and we were learning how to walk, we showed persistence. We fell down time and time again. But we kept getting up until we succeeded and learned to walk. We did the same thing when we learned to talk. And again the same thing when we learned to ride a bicycle. We owe much of our progress in life to persistence.

As we get older we tend to use this persistence less and less. Other things get in our way. We place a great deal of importance on what other people think of us, what other people will say. We allow our self-worth to come from outside of ourselves rather than from within. We place more importance in other people's opinion of us than on our own opinion of ourselves. We become dependent on their approval.

We even allow what we *think* other people think of us to influence our opinion of ourselves to such a point that we develop a negative self-concept. When we were little children and we fell down, we did not let that stop us. If we show this same kind of persistence as grown-ups we cannot lose.

In Illinois many years ago, there was a young man who failed in business. He then ran for the legislature and was badly defeated. He went into business again. It too failed and he spent seventeen years of his life paying up the debts of a partner. His sweetheart died and he had a nervous breakdown. He entered politics again and ran for Congress and was again badly defeated. He then failed in an attempt to get an appointment to the United States Land Office. After that, he ran for the United States Senate and was badly defeated. Two years later he tried again and was also badly defeated. He had one failure after another. He could have easily given up and had a perfect alibi for why he did not do more with his life—for why he appeared to be so unsuccessful. But he persisted, and he became one of the greatest men in history. His name was Abraham Lincoln. Lincoln accepted himself, even though many people considered him as being stupid, ugly, and a total failure. He knew he wasn't perfect, but he knew he had potential and he kept going through the setbacks to self-actualization. He accepted other people. He cared about others, and he dedicated his life to helping other people. He was goal oriented, and he persisted. He was successful, even when he appeared to be a failure. Each setback was an opportunity to learn, grow, and develop his good qualities. There are no losers—just people who quit too soon.

Calvin Coolidge had this to say about persistence: "Nothing in the world can take the place of persistence. Talent will not; nothing is more common than unsuccessful men with talent. Genius will not; unrewarded genius is almost a proverb. Education will not; the world is full of educated derelicts. Persistence and determination alone are omnipotent. The slogan 'press on' has solved and always will solve the problems of the human race."

Here are some success statements to strengthen your persistence:

- ☐ **I enjoy staying with a project from beginning to end.**

- ☐ **I have great perseverance.**

- ☐ **I am naturally persistent.**

- ☐ **I am determined and persistent.**

- ☐ **I see it through.**

❏ **I now finish what I start.**

❏ **I focus my mind on a goal until it is achieved.**

**8.** *Program for your goals at least three times a day.* And in doing so, feel as though the desired end result has already taken place. Be thankful. This, of course, is the application of the second reel of your Mental Movie technique. (You'll remember that the first reel is used only once.)

As a reminder to use this step, stick a little note on your clock radio or nearby saying: "Take a few moments to program for your goal—*now!*"

For example, if your goal is to give a good speech, relax your mind and body in the usual way, and using that second reel project forward in time, and imagine you are already presenting the material effectively, enjoying the experience thoroughly. You are focusing on getting the message to the audience so it is understandable and usable, instead of focusing on yourself, trying to impress them with your presentation, or being concerned with their reactions. You are successfully accomplishing your goal and purpose and enjoying the process. Your presentation is well organized and prepared. You have an introduction, a body, and a conclusion. You are making good eye contact and mentally projecting "I love you" to all the people you are speaking to, whether one or one thousand. As you project love to them and focus on your purpose, you automatically lose self-consciousness and are more natural and spontaneous, which makes the presentation effective.

# Short- , Medium- , and Long-Range Goals

Some of your goals will require more time to accomplish than others. Therefore, you will have:

Short-Range Goals — Those that you believe can be attained from within a few days to within a few weeks.

Medium-Range Goals — Those that you believe will require between a few weeks to a year to attain.

Long-Range Goals — Those that you believe will take a year or more to attain.

Your short-range goals will sometimes be steps leading to medium- or long-range goals. Although you may want to have a million dollars, you could find that setting a goal to have it within a few weeks is unbelievable to you if, at the moment, your net worth is something like $1.85. However, a short-range goal of a lesser amount would be quite believable, as would be the million dollars as a long-range goal. Belief is very important. If you don't believe you can attain a goal, you probably won't. If you do believe you can do it, you can. As Richard Bach said in his book *Illusions*, "You are never given a wish without also being given the ability to make it come true...." You may have to work for it, however. (How to turn work into fun is covered in chapter 6.) Your goals need not be believable to other people, but they must be to you.

# How to Write Your Goals

The following eight steps for writing a goal have been effective for thousands of people. If you choose to write your goals on eight-and-one-half-inch paper, you will find that you will only require two pages to complete the eight steps. (On pages 119–120, you'll see an example of a written goal using these eight steps.)

1. State your goal.

2. Starting date.

3. Attainment date.

4. Rewards.

5. Starting point.

6. Plan.

7. Obstacles.

8. Solutions to obstacles.

**1.** *State your goal.* After reviewing your list of things that you would like to be, gain, possess, or accomplish in any area of life, choose one thing that you would most like to realize in the next few days to few weeks if it's a short-range goal, the next few weeks to a year for a medium-range goal, or the next year or more for a long-range goal.

When you review your list, it's possible that you may discover that everything you wrote on that list realistically will take much longer than a year. How do you use this list to help you select a short- or medium-range goal? For example, if you wrote that you'd like to take off one hundred pounds, you may not be ready to accept that you can do that in less than a year. If so, your goal could be a step leading to that end result. Let's say fifty pounds. Then you could make one hundred pounds your long-range goal. Or if you wrote that you would like to have a college degree, but all you have now is a high school diploma, your medium-range goal would be to complete a quarter or a semester in college.

**2.** *Starting date.* _____ The sooner you start, the sooner you'll get there. So why not start now?

**3.** *Attainment date.* You will achieve this goal by the following date: _____. Although you may achieve your goal a little sooner or later than this date, you will find that having a target date to shoot for will alert your body chemistry to take action, thereby helping you to avoid procrastination, and be more efficient.

**4.** *Rewards.* List the rewards that you will receive when you reach your goal. Imagine, visualize, feel, and enjoy the achievement of these rewards at least three times a day. This is one of the most enjoyable parts of goal setting. Getting a college degree may not be all that exciting if you just think of that piece of paper itself. However, if you focus on the rewards, it can be very exciting.

Here are some examples of rewards you may experience as a result of attaining the goal of a college degree: The job you may be able to get, which you might not be able to get without that degree. The income you may enjoy that you may not receive without that degree. The admiraation and respect you get from family and friends for having accomplished something that required so much time, energy, and money. The sense of fulfillment, satisfaction, or achievement you will enjoy as a result of this accomplishment. This is where your programming comes in. You relax your mind the usual way and dwell on the positive end result, the accomplishment of this goal. And you allow yourself to feel as though it's already happening. You feel good as you are focusing on the reward while programming, and you are setting up patterns in your mind for future success.

5. *Starting point.* Begin with the initiation date—the date you are writing the goal. Describe your starting point. Where are you in relation to where you want to go? This is an important step for two reasons. First, it serves as a record of where you are starting. This helps you to measure your progress. Often when we look back at a goal we wrote a year or two ago, we are amazed to find how far we have come and how much we have accomplished. Our progress has seemed so natural that we forget where we started. When we read a goal that was written a year or two ago, we become aware of how far we have come. And our present success is something we chose, something we created.

This realization helps us improve. Then we are inspired to set more goals. Another important reason for this step is that it helps us to see the current situation more clearly. It helps us define the problem. And defining the problem is often considered to be 90 percent of the problem-solving process.

6. *Plan.* Write down steps you will take to achieve this goal. At this point it's a good idea to do a little individual brainstorming. Write any steps you could possibly take to achieve the goal. Do not be critical of these steps at this stage. Just write down whatever comes to mind. Later, when you review the steps, you may decide there are some you will choose to discard. But there will be some that you will decide are quite valuable.

You can then take action as you continue to program daily for your goal. You will find that as you are dwelling on your positive end result in a relaxed state of mind, ideas will often come to you on steps you can take to bring about this end result. You will find that these ideas help motivate you to do whatever is necessary to achieve your goals. When these ideas come to you, include them in your written plan along with the steps you've already written.

7. *Obstacles.* List all possible obstacles that you may encounter. Include anything that may hinder you in reaching your goal. It may seem negative to mention obstacles, but obstacles are not necessarily negative. It depends on what we do with them. If we write down the obstacles and take a good hard look at each one, we may find that the obstacles don't exist.

For example, you may say, "I want to get into better physical condition. But I just don't have the time right now." When you write this down and really think about it, you'll realize that getting yourself in better physical condition does not take much time each day. If you really want it, you'll find the time. And you will find that very soon your improved physical condition is accompanied by a sense of well-being. You think more clearly and have greater energy to do many more things, too. Consequently, exercising can actually save you time by increasing your efficiency and productivity, thereby assisting you in attaining and maintaining greater prosperity.

There may be time when you encounter an obstacle that truly is formidable. When this occurs, *welcome that obstacle.* Studies have shown that people who set goals, write them down, and work their plan, and encounter no obstacles, achieve the goal as originally stated. That makes sense, doesn't it? If we write the goal, work the plan, and encounter no obstacles, of course we're going to achieve the goal. However, those people who encounter obstacles along the way and persist, not only achieve their goal as originally stated but they go far beyond what they originally stated.

Obstacles are often advantages or opportunities—even blessings in disguise. In fact, TK, the Chinese word for *crisis*, has two characters. One of them means opportunity. And in *Illusions*, Richard Bach says, "There is no such thing as a problem without a gift in its hands."

I haven't always seen it that way, however. Many years ago I gave up very easily when faced with an obstacle. I was easily defeated. Since then I've learned that obstacles can force creativity and greater use of one's potential—a most important lesson.

Some of my students have told me that they have become so optimistic that now when they encounter an obstacle or get some "bad" news concerning their goals, they automatically say, "Oh good!" Then they immediately start looking for something positive in the situation. They say that every time they do this they inevitably find that the "bad" news turned out to be an advantage or opportunity. What, at first, seemed to be the worst thing that could have happened, actually became the best thing that could have happened. I've tried the same approach when faced with "disastrous" news, and it worked the same for me.

**8.** *Solutions to obstacles.* List solutions to possible obstacles. Approach each obstacle with the feeling that you already have a good solution. Again, many times, if not always, great opportunities arise when we encounter obstacles, and these opportunities and solutions become more apparent when you maintain a positive attitude and take time to analyze the situation or obstacle in a relaxed state of mind.

Perhaps you will agree with Booker T. Washington's statement regarding the overcoming of obstacles: "Success is to be measured not so much by the position that one has reached in life, as by the obstacles which he has overcome while trying to succeed."

You'll find that it only takes about ten minutes to write a goal using this formula. With each goal you write, the process becomes easier and more enjoyable. Keep in mind that we are goal-striving mechanisms. We are built to solve problems. We function best when we are striving toward a goal.

# Example of a Written Goal

1. State your goal: _Double My Income Within 12 Months_

2. Starting date: _Jan 1st_
3. Attainment date: _Dec 31st_

4. List the rewards:

I can pay off my debts
I can buy a new car.
I can take the vacation I've
been dreaming about

5. Determine your starting point:

My income is now $_____

6. Make a plan:

I will reject negative thoughts, images & feelings
I will now replace them with the appropriate affirmation
I will now use the Mental Movie technique at least
twice a day, and visualize myself having achieved
my goal. I will see myself as happy --- enjoying
the rewards listed above.
I will release my creativity & motivation
through the use of my affirmation and
mental images and feelings of success.
I will turn work into fun and do whatever
is necessary to succeed with pleasure. This
will give me the energy & enthusiasm to
provide a better product & service and gain
cooperation from coworkers & customers.

## 7. Examine obstacles (if any):

1. Doubts & fear of failure.
2. Feelings of unworthiness.
3. Lack of time to do the things necessary to double my income.


## 8. List possible solutions and advantage of obstacles:

1. Doubts & fears will be overcome, initially by my affirmations & mental imagery, and before long, by my successful experiences --- which will lead to my new more positive reality of being a prosperous person who deserves, and will have, even more success.

2. I will become so motivated by programming for my goals with my affirmations and visualization techniques that I will 1) have more energy to do what needs to be done. And it will seem more like fun than work,
2) drop those things from my schedule that no longer seem important or enjoyable compared to my goals,
3) become more efficient and productive so I can accomplish more in less time,
4) I will make time to do what has to be done!

## FORMS FOR YOUR GOALS

You may use the following pages to write a short-, a medium-, and a long-range goal, or you can use separate sheets of paper and remember to cover all eight steps.

### Short-Range Goal #1

**1. State your goal:** _____

_____

**2. Starting date:** _____

**3. Attainment date:** _____

**4. List the rewards:**

**5. Determine your starting point:**

**6. Make a plan:**

**7. Examine obstacles (if any):**




**8. List possible solutions and advantage of obstacles:**

# Medium-Range Goal #1

1. State your goal: _____

_____

2. Starting date: _____

3. Attainment date: _____

4. List the rewards:

5. Determine your starting point:

6. Make a plan:

**7. Examine obstacles (if any):**

**8. List possible solutions and advantage of obstacles:**

# Long-Range Goal #1

**1. State your goal:** _____

_____

**2. Starting date:** _____

**3. Attainment date:** _____

**4. List the rewards:**

**5. Determine your starting point:**

**6. Make a plan:**

**7. Examine obstacles (if any):**




**8. List possible solutions and advantage of obstacles:**

# CHAPTER 6

# SAVING

# AND

# INVESTMENT

# TIPS

*Almost anyone knows how to earn money, but not one in a million knows how to spend it.*

Henry David Thoreau

Now that you know how important and easy it is to set goals, I highly recommend that you write some goals that will help you to save money and invest it wisely. The information in this chapter will assist you in achieving those goals.

## SAVING

Almost every book or article on investments recommends that you save at least 10 percent of what you earn, and I agree. But you may ask, how do I save 10 percent of my income when up to now my income has been inadequate to pay my bills?

Good question. And there is more than one good answer.

First of all, if you continue to apply the strategies and techniques presented in this book, you will soon see a substantial increase in your income, very likely much more than 10 percent. In fact, it may double, triple, or quadruple within a few years. I know people who have done far better than that in far less time by using what has been offered to you in these pages. The key word here is "using." The strategies and techniques will only help you if you use them.

Secondly, you can save a tremendous amount of money by spending more wisely. How can you do this? Become aware that when you are paid to work you are giving up a part of your life energy in exchange for the money you are earning. Therefore, you are paying for whatever you spend your money on with a part of your life. When you think of it that way, you are likely to spend your money more wisely. Make it a point to think of this before you spend. You will surely find that some of the things you have been buying are definitely worth the price of your life energy. Just as surely, you will decide that some of the things you have been purchasing are not worth the portion of your life that was (or will be) required to accumulate the money needed to pay for it.

Some of your purchases may be out of habit. You may not be getting the same if any gratification from spending your money these ways. For example: When I was in college my wardrobe was almost nonexistent. I had no money for clothes. After graduation I began earning some money and bought a couple of suits, a sport coat, some shirts, and shoes. Each item of clothing provided me with a full measure of gratification. It felt great to have some nice clothes. To me these purchases were worth the life energy I was trading for them.

In recent years, however, I have found myself buying clothes even though I have little or no need for additional clothing and I get very little gratification from each purchase. So before buying I now ask myself, "Is this product or service worth the piece of my life energy

I must give in order to have it?" If the answer is "yes," I feel very good about spending my money this way. However, often the answer is "no." Consequently I am able to avoid making purchases that bring me little or no gratification.

Please notice that by doing this I am not depriving myself. I am freeing myself to use my money for whatever will bring me greater gratification.

Try this yourself. You'll be amazed how much money you can save by asking yourself "Is this worth the portion of my life energy I must give in exchange?" When you determine that something is not worth the cost of the piece of your life you must pay for it, you are then free to use that money in a way or ways that you decide is better. You may use it to pay off debts, buy something that you *really* want or need, or invest it so you will have much more for whatever you need or want in the future.

## INVESTMENTS

The value of investing money is to get it working for you. The more your money works for you, the less of your life energy is needed to acquire money. Along with the other tools in this book for attracting money, if you save and invest wisely you will eventually become financially independent. You can then live on the return of your investments without reducing the principal. In other words, if you decide you require $20,000 a year to cover your living expenses, and you have $200,000 invested which is yielding 10 percent (equaling $20,000) you are currently financially independent. However, you must also factor in inflation. If the inflation rate is 5 percent, and all else remains the same, the amount you need for living expenses will also increase by 5 percent per year.

Therefore, you will need a larger amount invested or you will need a higher return on your investment.

Once you are financially independent it is no longer necessary to work for money. You can do whatever you please. You may decide to work, but it won't be because you *need* the money.

Since your continued financial independence will depend on investing wisely, let's talk about some methods of investment. To begin with, it is very important to invest your money so it will earn the highest possible return without undue risk to your capital. Before offering you some tips on investing I want to re-emphasize that it is vital to use what you've learned in this book and keep in mind that you *deserve* to have continued prosperity through your investments.

Many years ago, before I learned the techniques and strategies I've shared with you in this book, I worked very hard and managed to accumulate a fairly large amount of money. However, my self-image was still so negative that when I invested this money in the stock market, somehow I would choose stocks that would immediately proceed to go down by 20 percent or more. Some companies went completely out of business within months after my stock purchase. It was uncanny! My more sadistic friends found this amusing and begged me to tell them which stocks I was buying so they could sell those same stocks short.

What was happening here? How could my choices be so poor, even when I followed the advice of professional investment "gurus"? The odds against anyone picking stocks so poorly by pure chance would be astronomical.

I believe that I was somehow psychically making poor choices because at some level of consciousness I didn't feel I deserved to have more than a very small

amount of financial success, and when I exceeded that
level I would sabotage myself to bring me back to the
level that was "right" for me.

Fortunately, I have developed my prosperity consciousness to where I now have excellent results with
my investments.

Even when you have overcome poverty consciousness, it is still necessary to pay close attention to what
you do with your savings. In this way you will be able to
do the things you feel are most worthwhile and enjoyable for the rest of your life without having to worry
about money.

In the process of investigating various forms of
investments such as real estate, stocks, bonds, gold,
CD's, money market funds and other mutual funds, I
have become aware of, and subscribed to, many financial
advisory newsletters. The majority of them state, and I
agree, that the best way for most people to invest in
stocks is through mutual funds. But these advisory
services offer conflicting advice as to which funds to buy
and sell, and while some are optimistic and advise you
to buy, others are saying to sell and invest in money
market funds or short term U.S. treasury securities. It
took me years to weed out those services whose track
records were much poorer than their hyped-up advertis-
ing would lead you to believe. To do this by trial and
error can be very expensive.

A better way to do it is to subscribe to a service
like the *Hulbert Financial Digest* which will provide
you with objective ratings of over 130 financial newsletters. *HFD* reports the year-to-date performance, and com-
pares the previous 36 months' performance of each
portfolio recommended in these newsletters to the Wilshire
5,000's total return. As its name indicates, the Wilshire
5,000 tracks the prices of 5,000 different stocks, and is

much broader than the Dow Jones average, which includes only 30 blue chip stocks.

*HFD* also evaluates the riskiness of each newsletter. This is important because some financial newsletters may have had good results but their recommended investments may be too risky for your purposes. For example, if you are retired or close to retirement you are probably more interested in safe, conservative investments that protect your capital and provide you with a reliable income than you are in investments that have growth potential but at a high risk.

Each January and July issue of *HFD* reports the long-term performance, as well as the current data, for every year they have tracked each newsletter since 1980. To get a sample or subscription information write to: Hulbert Financial Digest, 316 Commerce Street, Alexandria, VA 22314; or phone: (703) 683-5905.

After you have found one or more financial newsletters that you like, you will have a good start toward making wise decisions with your investment money. Even if you choose to hire a professional to manage your investment portfolio rather than do it yourself, you will find that the information you acquire in these newsletters will help you to communicate your investment philosophy and ideas to a money manager and you will be better able to evaluate the job your manager is doing for you.

If you don't have the time or desire to manage your own portfolio of investments, a good money manager can be worth his/her weight in gold. Some are so knowledgeable and conscientious they will help you to realize a much higher rate of return on your money than you are likely to achieve on your own. But even so, it's a good idea to stay on top of your investments and get monthly, or at least quarterly, statements. In fact, you should insist that no purchase or sale be made without your written approval. I know of some people who have lost all their savings by giving total control to a money manager and ignoring what that manager was doing until it was too late.

Historically the best investments have been (1) your own business (provided you are well prepared to go into that business), (2) your own home and other real estate (although in recent years homes, and real estate in general have not appreciated in value as they have in the past, especially during the 1960s and 1970s), (3) mutual funds, and (4) stocks.

For people who don't have their own business, and for those who do but have additional money to invest, I believe mutual funds represent the best form of investment. The advantage of buying mutual funds over individual stocks or bonds is diversification. The success of your investment isn't dependent upon the success of one company, or one industry for that matter, unless you invest in sector funds. A sector stock fund consists of stocks of only one industry, such as gold or electronics, and is much less diversified and generally more risky than funds that include stocks from many industries.

You can invest in mutual funds that have a sales charge, called a load, or you could purchase a no-load fund, and pay no sales charge. Since research shows that load funds do not outperform no-load funds, it makes sense to invest in the no-load funds that suit your investment objectives and have the best performance records, not just for the past year but over a period of three, five, or ten years. Another advantage with mutual funds is that you have a professional management team to analyze and determine which stocks and bonds to buy or sell.

If you invest in a fund that is part of a family of no-load funds that includes a money market fund such as Vanguard, T. Rowe Price, or Scudder, and at some point you decide that the outlook for stocks is not good, with just a telephone call you can sell your stock fund and have your money put in the safer money market fund where it will earn interest until the outlook for stocks improves. When it does, you can phone in your order to transfer the funds into the fund in that family that seems most appealing to you. You could also redeem your shares in the funds of one family and purchase a fund outside of that family, or use it for another investment.

But how do you know when to have your money in a stock or bond fund and when to have it in a money market fund? I don't know of anyone who knows for sure what the market will do on any given day, but I have learned a rule of thumb that has helped me decide where my money should be, and I think you will find this very helpful.

The rule of thumb is: When the Federal Reserve (the Fed) now headed by Alan Greenspan establishes a trend of lowering interest rates, stock and bond funds (most, if not all) will go up. When the Federal Reserve establishes a trend of increasing interest rates, stock and bond funds (most, if not all) will go down. I consider a trend established if the Fed raises rates twice in a row, and do not consider a new trend established until the Fed decides to lower rates two consecutive times.

If you have chosen good stock or bond funds you will get the greatest return on your investment by keeping your money there while interest rates are in a downward trend, and moving to a money market fund when rates begin an upward trend.

The main thing is to keep your money working for you in the best possible way, and you will be better able to do this if you are well informed and feel that you *deserve* it.

# CHAPTER 7

# QUICK TIPS FOR SUCCESSFUL LIVING

*If you are pained by an external thing, it is not this thing that disturbs you, but your own judgment about it; and it is in your power to wipe out this judgment now.*

Marcus Aurelius

For many years, I have been searching for words of wisdom offered throughout history by people whose lives have generally been regarded as successful. In this chapter, you are offered some of the most valuable ideas, techniques, and tips for successful living that I have been able to acquire. They will supplement and support the techniques presented in previous chapters to assist you in attaining both financial success and peace of mind.

These acquired gems of wisdom have been blended with my own thoughts and discoveries on the subjects based on applying them in my own life, and observing the benefits derived by many other people who have tested these concepts in their lives. Although more space could be devoted to each subject, sometimes it is more practical and effective to have information presented in a condensed version. With this in mind, I offer you quick tips for successful living regarding the following subjects:

- How to deal with worry
- How to be happy and healthy, now
- Handling criticism
- Overcoming procrastination
- Having more good luck
- Getting whatever you want
- Developing your natural enthusiasm
- Developing a preference for wealth—not an addiction
- Recognizing the importance and joy of giving with love

## How to Deal with Worry

*The reason worry kills more people
than work is that
more people worry than work.*

Robert Frost

Just about everyone has done some worrying, but few are aware of the process we go through when we worry. Here is what happens: We picture a negative end result in our mind, and this does not take any effort or willpower. We just dwell on it, and in a short time this negative end result appears very real to us, and we are generating the appropriate emotions that go along with the negative end result, such as fear, anxiety, discouragement. Consequently, we are feeling bad right now and we are suffering right now for something that is merely a thought in our mind. In addition to that, we are setting up patterns in our mind for future negative end results. Even if the event never actually happens, the worry takes its toll through immediate discomfort and the harmful effects of excessive stress. It is said that worry is interest paid in advance on a debt you may never owe. Mark Twain said, "I've had a lot of problems in my day...most of which never happened." Calvin Coolidge put it this way: "If you see ten troubles coming down the road, you can be sure that nine will run into the ditch before they reach you."

Now suppose we change that negative end result to a positive. We are now picturing a positive end result in our mind. This, too, takes very little effort or will-power, particularly after you have practiced doing it for a while. In no time at all we will be generating the proper emotions that go along with that positive end result, and we will be feeling good, right now, for something that is merely a thought in our mind. We will be feeling happiness and joy, plus we'll be setting up patterns in our mind for future success.

All we have done here is that we have taken the worry process, which all of us have experienced many, many times, and we have changed the end result to something positive. After practicing this for a while, we will find it just as easy to focus on positive end results as it is to worry.

We don't have to force ourselves to worry. People don't say, "Oh boy, look at what time it is. I'm way behind on my worrying," or, "I've just got to do some more worrying."

We do not schedule our worry, although that would be a good idea. Napoleon Hill, the great author and motivator who worked with Thomas Edison, used to schedule his worry for Friday afternoon. If he found himself worrying on Monday or Tuesday, he would write it in on the schedule for Friday afternoon. When Friday afternoon came around, it seemed there was nothing to worry about. Those things had taken care of themselves.

We could also apply the law of reverse effect, which is the experience of getting the opposite results of what we are trying very hard to do. For example, when we try very hard to remember something we often find it becomes more illusive, more difficult to remember. When we try very hard not to be nervous, we seem to become more nervous. When we try very hard to visualize something, we often draw a blank, and if we try very hard to worry, we often find there is nothing to worry about.

We have all had so much practice worrying we probably could be considered experts. Nevertheless, if we try very hard to worry, we often find there is nothing to worry about. We just draw a blank.

You might even consider participating in some worry competition. You could invite your friends over and see who can outdo the other with worrisome comments. This could easily result in genuine, cathartic laughter, and a more positive perspective. If they refuse to participate, you could do a worry demonstration. You could say, "Do you want to see some championship worrying? Watch this!"

Another way to deal with worry is to turn the negative into a positive. As soon as you find yourself worrying about something, let it serve as a triggering device to project positive images, a reminder to dwell on the positive end results. As you continue to do this, you will find that you will worry less and less.

## Some Additional Thoughts on Worry

- Bertrand Russell said, "Worry is a form of fear, and all forms of fear produce fatigue. A man who has learned not to feel fear will find the fatigue of daily life enormously diminished."

- Dr. Charles Mayo said, "Worry affects circulation, the heart, the glands, the whole nervous system, and profoundly affects the health."
- Shakespeare said, "There is nothing either good or bad, but thinking makes it so."
- Alfred Adler said, "We are influenced not by 'facts,' but by our interpretation of facts."
- Richard Mathison in his book *What Dreams May Come* said, "Your body has an alarm system to meet emergencies. This alarm system produces a super-energy to use and burn during an emergency. If the emergency is *real*, you use up that energy.

  "But worry is an imagined emergency in the future. From the neck down, your body can't seem to tell a real emergency from an imagined one, so it goes into an alarm state and generates the super-energy. Since your situation doesn't exist yet, there is no place to spend energy—no cougar to kill. Controlling all of that super-energy is hard work, it causes wear and tear on the body, leaving us in a diseased condition. That which you believe becomes your world."

Recommended Success Statements:

❑ **I replace negative thoughts with positives.**

❑ **I am now positive and optimistic.**

❑ **I expect things to turn out well.**

❑ **I am enjoying peace of mind.**

☐ **I let go of worry.**

☐ **I allow myself to feel carefree.**

☐ **I have a positive outlook.**

## How to Be Happy and Healthy, Now

*If you get up every day saying, 'What do I have to give the world,' you'll never have a problem defining yourself and being happy. As soon as you see the world with loving eyes, it changes.*

Bernard Siegel, M.D.

Most of us postpone happiness. We say, "I'll be happy when this happens," or "I'll be happy if that happens." For example, "I'll be happy if I pass the test." "I'll be happy if I get an A in the course." "I'll be happy when I graduate." "I'll be happy if I get a job." "I'll be happy if I get a raise." "I'll be happy when I get married." "I'll be happy when I get a divorce."

Most of us say that something must happen before we're to be happy. Consequently, we never fully experience happiness regardless of our financial condition. As I stated earlier, the purpose of this book is not just to help you attract money, but to enjoy life more completely.

The only way I know of to be assured of being happy in the future is to be happy now. Some people may say, "But there are many things in my life that I am not happy about now, and I want to see them changed." And that is probably true for all of us, and it probably always will be so, but our tendency is to focus on minor annoyances and to overlook the positives in our lives.

For example, when do we really appreciate health? When we are sick. When we are sick, health is everything. Money is nothing compared to health if you are really hurting. But when we are healthy, do we really think about it? Do we really enjoy it?

Now that I am aware of this, I take a little time each day to appreciate my good health. When I am feeling good, I am more aware of it; and I say to myself, "I feel good, I feel healthy, and this is the way I am going to continue to feel, and even better in the future." By doing this, I am enjoying that present moment more completely, plus I am programming for more good health in the future. I am establishing a point of reference for good health, and this seems to help me to feel the same way in the future.

When do we really appreciate loved ones? When they are far away, or when they are dead. But did we fully appreciate them when they were with us? I now more fully enjoy people that I love when I am with them because I know that those particular moments will never come again. I build up good memories in my mind that I can relive again in the future if I choose to do so.

Many years ago my two youngest sons, Bob and Jeff, had just walked out of the front door of our house. The office in my home has a window that looks out onto the front lawn, and I saw them walking along with their arms around each other, talking. Here were two little boys, one eight, one seven, who were obviously good friends. It was a touching, beautiful moment for me, and at the time I thought, "Someday I will wish I could go back in time and reexperience this moment." So I decided to get the most out of that particular moment. I enjoyed it thoroughly, and I made such a deep impression that, as I'm sharing it with you now, I can reexperience that moment vividly.

How about freedom? Do we really appreciate being free? There are people in many parts of the world who are not free. They would give anything for the freedom we enjoy but seldom think about. I taught a class recently at the state prison in Saint Cloud, Minnesota, (was there really a saint by the name of Cloud?), and the main thing on the minds of those men was freedom.

When was the last time you thought about your freedom? We are living in perhaps the freest country in the world, with great opportunities, plenty of food and shelter. We have so much to be happy about, and yet our tendency is to be unhappy, to dwell on the negatives, even though they are small compared to the positives.

Why not make up your mind right now to be happy *right now*? Why not enjoy each moment, each event, each person? Be thankful for what you have and who you are each day. This will focus your thoughts on abundance and make it much easier for you to experience happiness and prosperity in the future.

A key to happiness is to change your addictions to preferences. When we have addictions, we always seem to want more, and if we always want more, we will never have enough. It is okay for us to prefer to have a certain thing happen, but if it doesn't happen, we can continue to be happy because it is not a condition for our happiness. If it does happen, great. But if it doesn't happen, we will go on being happy.

Recommended Success Statements:

☐ **I choose to be happy *now!***
☐ **I smile and laugh easily.**
☐ **I see the positive side of all situations.**

❑ **Life is fun and I enjoy it.**

❑ **I live each moment to the fullest.**

❑ **I feel happy and carefree.**

❑ **I count my blessings.**

# HANDLING CRITICISM

*No one can make you feel inferior
without your permission.*

Eleanor Roosevelt

The fear of being criticized keeps most people
from asking questions, trying new things, and expressing
themselves freely. It also causes excessive stress and
prevents people from developing their potential. Fear of
criticism also limits our ability to attain and enjoy
prosperity. It can cause us to abandon (or never even
begin) projects that would be very profitable and fulfilling.

If you have been having a difficult time handling
criticism, try looking at it this way. If the criticism is
valid, you can learn from it. You can grow and make
some positive changes. You now know something about
yourself or your behavior that you can correct. Prior to
that time, you may not have been aware of the problem,
and it could have stayed with you indefinitely. Therefore
you have gained, and can be thankful. In fact, you may
decide to thank the person who offers the criticism.

If, however, after objectively examining the criticism you decide that it is not valid, there is no reason for
you to be upset because it is the other person's problem,
not yours. If you allow it to upset you, then you make
the problem yours. You will then be allowing that per-

son to control you. The more you build a strong, positive self-image, the more open you will be to criticism. You will find it cannot hurt you, and it can often help you.

It is important to build yourself so strong through the Mental Movie, affirmations, and other programming techniques offered in this book that the criticism is not a threat to your self-worth. You will benefit from placing more importance on your own positive opinion of yourself than negative statements offered by others.

Another important way to handle criticism successfully is to recognize that you do not need everyone's approval. No one throughout history has been free of criticism. No one has received unanimous approval.

Although knowledgeable people will usually rate Bach and Beethoven as two of the greatest composers in history, millions of people will not even listen to their music. They think it is terrible. Millions of people think Shakespeare's plays are boring. Perhaps most people would say, "Turn that noise off," if they heard a recording of Caruso and other great (my adjective) singers.

Who is your favorite singer? Frank Sinatra, Bing Crosby, Luciano Pavarotti, Barbra Streisand, Whitney Houston, Elvis Presley? Millions will disagree with you. Who is your favorite comedian? Bob Hope, Carol Burnett, Groucho Marx, Woody Allen, Joan Rivers, Richard Pryor, Billy Crystal, Gallagher, Steve Martin? You probably won't have to look far to find someone who thinks that one of these people, or all of them, are not at all funny. Although Muhammad Ali and Ted Williams had millions of fans, millions of others didn't like them at all. As successful as the Beatles were, there were many millions who didn't enjoy them. When U.S. presidential candidates have won by a landslide, they still had 40 percent of the voters voting against them. And there were millions of others who weren't impressed enough even to go to the polls. Perhaps the ultimate example of a mixture of approval and disapproval is to be found in the life and crucifixion of Jesus Christ. Can any of us really expect 100 percent approval? Do we really need it?

The point here is that although other people have a right to their opinion, you certainly *do not have to agree with them*. Approval is nice to have, but you don't need it (except from yourself).

## A Final Thought on Handling Criticism

A man met him on the street one day and began to call him mean and ugly names. Buddha listened quietly and thoughtfully until the man ran out of epithets, and had to pause for breath.

"If you offer something to a man and he refuses it, to whom does it belong?" asked Buddha.

The spiteful man replied, "It belongs, I suppose, to the one who offered it."

Then Buddha said, "The abuse and vile names you offer me, I refuse to accept."

The detractor turned and walked away.

Recommended Success Statements:

❑ **I am now free of the fear of criticism.**

❑ **I have nothing to fear.**

❑ **I have high self-esteem.**

❑ **I am positive and confident.**

❑ **Valid criticism helps me—invalid criticism is rejected.**

❏ **I handle criticism successfully.**

❏ **My self-worth comes from within.**

# Overcoming Procrastination

*This book is a victory over my own*
*procrastination.*

Bob Griswold

Many of us say we procrastinate too much. We put off doing things that we feel we should be doing. This is often due to the idea that we must do things perfectly. We may set such high standards for a project that it seems impossible to complete it properly. Out of fear of failure we find ways to postpone the task. This can lead to feelings of guilt and harsh criticism of ourselves, which make us feel even less capable of accomplishing the task, and the procrastination continues.

A good way to deal with procrastination is to set a minigoal. That is, set a goal to work at it for fifteen minutes, and once you've worked on it for fifteen minutes, you would have completed your goal and you can feel a sense of satisfaction for having accomplished that much. However, often by that time you will want to continue with what you have been doing, and you will go beyond your original goal.

You may even find yourself completing the entire task.

What we are doing here is activating the law of inertia, which is that when we are standing still it is difficult to get started, but once we are moving, it is easy to keep moving. Sometimes at the end of the fifteen-minute period, you will stop and do something else, but you won't feel bad about leaving the job. You may even choose to give yourself a little reward because you completed your minigoal. You did what you said you were going to do. And those times when you decide to complete the entire task, you will find that it doesn't seem like work. It is not something you should do, or have to do, it is something you want to do, and you feel even better once it is completed. It is said that life by the yard is hard; by the inch it's a cinch.

Recommended success statements:

- ❏ **I am a "do-it-now" person.**
- ❏ **I like to jump right in and get busy.**
- ❏ **I am loaded with energy for the task at hand.**
- ❏ **I do first things first.**
- ❏ **I am energetic, ambitious, and motivated.**
- ❏ **I take action now.**
- ❏ **I love to get started on projects, and stay with them.**

## HAVING MORE GOOD LUCK

*Chance favors the prepared mind.*

Louis Pasteur

The more you prepare yourself by practicing your techniques, finding what you love and doing it, the luckier you will be. Pay particular attention to your attitude regarding luck.

Do you say things like, "I'm not lucky," or "Just my luck," or "With my luck it will probably rain," or "With my luck we will probably lose"? Press the CLEAR button on such negative programming. A big step toward having more good luck is to make the choice to have it. Say to yourself several times each day, "I'm lucky," and allow yourself to *feel* lucky. One benefit you'll enjoy by doing this is you'll become more aware of things that probably would have happened anyway, which could be considered good luck. And with this awareness you'll enjoy those events much more. Another benefit of doing this is that you'll be more aware of opportunities. If you keep saying, "I'm lucky," an inner voice may be saying, "If I'm so lucky, where's the luck?" And you'll start looking around for it and you'll notice opportunities that you might not have noticed otherwise, and you'll be able to take advantage of those opportunities.

Another benefit is that you will create good luck for yourself. You'll make things happen. You'll create an aura about you that will be propitious to good luck or good fortune. We tend to bring into our reality those things that we hold in our mind. You deserve good luck as much as anyone; and if you choose it, you'll have it!

Recommended success statements:

❏ **My luck is improving daily.**

❏ **I create my own good luck.**

❏ **I am fortunate in many ways.**

❏ **I deserve good luck.**

❏ **I am now more aware of opportunities.**

❏ **Good things are coming my way.**

❏ **I am lucky.**

## GETTING WHATEVER YOU WANT

Although no two people have experienced exactly the same programming, there is at least one thing we all have been programmed to do. Knowing what that thing is and using it properly can help you to get whatever you want.

What is it that we have been programmed to do? Everyone has been programmed to comply when asked a question. From the time we were little babies we have been bombarded with questions, and we have been taught to give a favorable response to those questions. It is a learned or conditioned response. You can observe the process every day with little children. They are asked:

"What is your name?"
"Where is Daddy?"
"Who is that?"
"Can you smile for me?"
"What is this?"
"What do you want?"
"What color is this?"
"What does the dog say?"
"Do you want this?"
"Are you hungry?"

The programming to respond to questions intensifies when we go to school, and goes on day after day, week after week, year after year. We are *expected* to answer when asked questions that are not too personal or outrageous.

When we leave school and enter business, programming for a favorable response to asking continues. Whenever the boss asks us to do something, the learned response to comply is reinforced. By that time, and usually much earlier in life, we have developed an unconscious habit to almost automatically give a favorable response to any reasonable question.

You can take advantage of this knowledge and get wherever you want by properly asking for it. This doesn't mean that everyone you ask will do everything you ask them to do or give you everything you ask for. However, you will get the results you desire often enough to make you *much more successful and prosperous* than you would have been if you had not used this simple, but powerful technique.

Here are some examples:

- Ask for a discount or a good price. You will often get it.
- Ask for a favor. People (especially successful people) enjoy doing favors for someone who asks in a courteous and proper manner.
- Ask for a second or third opinion in medical matters so you may avoid unnecessary surgery, medication, and expense.
- Ask in selling. There are three things to ask:
    1. For the appointment.
    2. To get information about the prospect's needs and desires, so you can provide a better service.
    3. For the order. Countless sales are lost by people who forgot to ask for the order.
- Ask your teachers. They usually are favorably impressed by those who ask questions, and will help you to increase your knowledge. In college,

when I did poorly on a quiz, I asked where and why I was wrong, and asked for the correct answer. Learning from my mistakes by asking helped me get A's on the final exams.

- Ask for a raise in pay or a promotion. Although you may not get it immediately the likelihood that you eventually will is greatly increased by asking. You show your boss that you think your services are of more value than your current pay or position would indicate. He/she will then begin to think of you in those terms as well. Of course, when you ask for a raise or a promotion, it is a good idea to be prepared to explain why you think you deserve it.
- Ask for bids or quotes. I have found that some businesses charge as much as two or three times more than others for comparable products or services. Asking has saved me many thousands of dollars.
- Ask if you want to raise funds. Churches and charities would receive very little without asking.
- Ask for a date. That person may be hoping you will. As you build your self-image, any fears of rejection disappear.
- Ask yourself questions in a relaxed state of mind and listen . . . and you will discover that you have the answer to many, if not all, of your questions.
- Ask in prayer, and immediately believe your prayer is answered, and you will find it is.

For a complete examination of the power of asking, read *How to Get Whatever You Want* by M. R. Kopmeyer.

Think of some of the ways you can apply the power of asking in your life today. It is one of the most important techniques you will ever learn, but it is of no help unless you use it.

Recommended success statements:

❑ **I now find it easy to ask for what I want.**

❑ **It is okay for me to ask questions.**

❑ **I love to ask.**

❑ **I learn by asking.**

❑ **I profit by asking.**

❑ **People enjoy answering my questions.**

❑ **Asking helps me get what I deserve.**

## Developing Your Natural Enthusiasm

*Enthusiasts are fighters. They have fortitude. They have staying qualities. Enthusiasm is at the bottom of all progress! With it there is accomplishment; without it there are only alibis.*

Henry Ford

The English word *enthusiasm* derives from the Greek word *enthous,* which means "having a god within." And having a god within—a god with magiclike power—is what *enthusiasm* is all about.

Ralph Waldo Emerson said this about enthusiasm: "Every great and commanding moment in the annuls of this world is the triumph of some enthusiasm." He also said, "Enthusiasm is the power engine of success."

One of our greatest *natural* resources is *enthusiasm.* The word *natural* is emphasized because we all have it. We are born with it. We see so much of it in little children: they tingle with excitement, they show it with their entire bodies, they play, they shout, they bounce, they jump, they skip, they smile, they giggle, they laugh, they *live*.

When we allow our natural enthusiasm to surface, we *are* more alive. We are more interesting, more fun, and more productive.

How are we more productive? When we shed inhibitions, we can direct our energy toward our desired end results, and that energy seems unlimited when we are more enthusiastic. Whether it be in a work or social environment, people then find us more comfortable to be with, and we are more comfortable with them. Consequently we experience increased cooperation and a spirit of teamwork, which raises individual and organizational productivity.

We all have that naturally enthusiastic child within us, and we can release (or free) it, by getting back in touch with it at our basic programming level, and reliving some of the enthusiastic feelings we've had in the past.

The more we replay these feelings of enthusiasm, the more we set up patterns in our mind for enthusiasm for the future, and the more we overcome the habit of being overly subdued. In addition to this, you can program for enthusiasm by imaging yourself being enthusiastic in your daily activities. When programming first thing in the morning for a great day, imagine yourself greeting people enthusiastically, and as you are programming, *feel* the enthusiasm. Feel yourself "alive" and "turned on" in everything you do, and allow yourself to have the feelings of success and knowing that you are a winner, and then because of your enthusiasm, interest in others, and supportive attitude, anyone you deal with is also a winner.

Follow this up by *practicing* enthusiasm at the physical dimension. Notice the reaction you get from people when you greet them with a big smile and a bright, cheerful tone of voice, as if you're really happy to be alive. (Aren't you?) Life is *much* more fun when you *choose* to be happy to be alive.

Put the god within you to work. Practice being *enthusiastic*, and soon it will be as natural and as much fun for you as it was when you were little.

Recommended success statements:

☐ I *feel* enthusiastic.

☐ I am alive with energy and enthusiasm.

☐ I am positive, confident, and uninhibited.

☐ I am naturally enthusiastic.

☐ I express myself with positive emotions.

☐ I love to show my natural enthusiasm.

☐ My enthusiasm increases my prosperity.

## Developing a Preference for Wealth—Not an Addiction

You'll recall that the purpose of this book is not merely to help you attract money. It is to help you enjoy a happier, more fulfilling life as well. However, if you believe that in order to feel happy, secure, and worthwhile you must be wealthy, then you have a wealth addiction. An important key to happiness is to change this addiction to a preference.

It has been proven time and time again that if you prefer wealth and choose wealth, and you apply the principles presented here, it will soon be yours. Also, this wealth will blend with the other areas of life in a harmonious way and provide you with greater satisfaction, enjoyment, and fulfillment than if your desire for wealth were an addiction.

The problem with addictions is that we are never satisfied—never secure. We always seem to want more, and worry about losing what we have. By making prosperity a preference rather than an addiction, we have control over our self-worth. This helps us to function in more natural, relaxed, spontaneous, and creative ways, which in turn helps us toward our goal.

Jack Benny had a comic image of a man who was addicted to money. The man always wanted more and was very reluctant to part with what he had. In one of Benny's classic comedy scenes he was confronted by a man who stuck a gun in his back and said, "Your money or your life!" Benny just stood there and remained silent. The man raised his voice and repeated angrily, "I said, your money or your life!" Benny replied, *"I'm thinking!"* Although this is a very funny scene, such an addiction can be more tragic than comic.

Many years ago I worked with a man who was extremely wealthy. Unfortunately, he never truly enjoyed prosperity. He was addicted to money. In his mind he never seemed to have enough. He was so insecure in this respect that he virtually lived like a pauper in an attic apartment that was cluttered with debris. It was *very* difficult to walk anywhere in his apartment. He could have hidden a stack of thousand-dollar bills in the middle of his living room, and it would have been safe from burglars. Even if they knew it was there, they probably would never find it. They would get tired and give up the search.

When we had to drive somewhere on business, it

was not unusual for him to ask me to stop the car so he could get out to inspect an old tire or some other piece of junk he had spotted lying along the side of the road. Often he would lug these items home.

There were many other examples of his addiction, but I will share just one more with you. One afternoon we were sitting in a little café discussing a business deal. At one point in our discussion he wanted to illustrate a point on paper so he reached for a scratch pad that was on the table, and just as he was about to write something on it, he stopped abruptly, looked at the lunch counter across the room, and spotted some napkins. He quickly got up and retrieved a napkin after informing me, with kind of a sheepish grin, that he just couldn't see wasting a piece of scratch paper.

In describing this man's behavior, it is not my intention to ridicule or to be judgmental. He was operating from a state of awareness that resulted from his programming and choices over a period of many years. You or I might have acted similarly had we been walking in his shoes. Although I did not particularly admire some of his actions, there was no reason for me to dislike him because of it. Actually, I found much to like about the man. However, I eventually chose to discontinue doing business with him.

The point is that with such an addiction, a person misses out on some of the greatest joys in life. Acquiring money is exciting, but being able to use that money to purchase things that you need and want, and to share with others, is much more exciting and rewarding. Hopefully by this time this man has transformed his addiction to a preference and is enjoying better relationships, increased peace of mind, and the joy of spending and giving.

# RECOGNIZE THE IMPORTANCE AND JOY OF GIVING WITH LOVE

It is a basic law of life that we must give in order to receive. One of the main reasons that poverty is so prevalent is that most people expect something for nothing. We must sow before we reap.

Katherine Ponder says that if she "could shout only one message to the whole world regarding life's secrets it would be this: that you cannot get something for nothing, but that you can have the best of everything when you give full measure for the good you wish to receive." When people do not give or sow in any form in their life, they fail to make contact with the loving energy and great abundance available in the universe. As a result, they have no channel through which the unlimited wealth of the universe can pour forth its great riches to them.

So you don't have to wait until you are rich in order to start giving. The sooner you start the sooner you will begin attracting money. Everyone has something to give. If it isn't money or something material, it can be a service. It can be acceptance or empathy. It can be *love*. Doing someone a favor without expecting anything in return will reap benefits that will exceed the favor. When you smile and give sincere compliments and project love to others, you are sowing—you are forming a channel with the universe's rich, loving abundance.

In Glenn Clark's book about Walter Russell, *The Man Who Tapped the Secrets of the Universe*, he tells about Walter's teenage experience as a bellboy in a hotel. His salary was only $8 a month. But he was told he would receive about $100 in tips for the season.

However, when Walter's first tip was offered to him, something deep inside would not allow him to take it. He said, "No, thank you, sir," and quickly walked away. Walter immediately went to his retreat in the basement of the hotel and tried to understand why an inner voice had told him to refuse the tip. Suddenly he had a great inspiration. He said to himself, "I'll be the only bellboy in existence who never took a tip! And I'll be the *best* bellboy the world ever knew. I'll pledge myself to give the most joyful and cheerful service that ever a bellboy gave!"

From that moment on, Walter responded to every request very quickly. He was fast, courteous, and efficient. Every morning at 5:00 A.M. he would awaken and hurry to get cow's milk for a baby that needed special care and then he would go back to bed again. When people asked Walter why he did not accept tips, he replied, "I receive a salary, and I love my work." The hotel guests had never seen anything like this. They appreciated his attitude so much that they invited him on yachting trips and to dinner parties; and when the hotel management explained that it was against the rules for servants to socialize with guests, the influential guests told the management that if an exception was not made in his case they would never return again to that hotel. Walter had a very interesting and exciting summer.

Soon the guests became attracted to the sketching and painting Walter did during his spare time. At the end of the season, instead of receiving $100 from tips, he had received $850 for his paintings and five offers of legal adoption from wealthy families. Some of these people became lifelong friends, and from them and their friends, Walter received many commissions for his paintings once he became famous in that field. Incidentally,

Walter also went to the wedding of the baby for whom he got up at 5:00 A.M. to get the special milk.

Walter Russell was known to have said many times, "I have absolute faith that anything can come to one who trusts to the unlimited help of the Universal Intelligence, so long as one works within the law and always gives more to others than they expect, and does it cheerfully and courteously." This is not only an important principle for financial success, it is a formula for successful living—for being more human.

Giving people more than they expect also helps you feel that it is rightful for you to be prosperous. The more value you give, the more you will truly feel that you deserve all the money that you attract. You more than earned it. And feeling that you deserve money makes it much easier for you to attract it, to manage it well, and to fully enjoy it.

Recommended success statements:

☐ **I enjoy doing my best regardless of compensation.**

☐ **I get fulfillment from providing a good service.**

☐ **I enjoy giving.**

☐ **It is more blessed to give than to receive.**

☐ **I reap what I sow.**

☐ **I like to give more to others than they expect.**

☐ **I deserve the rewards that come from giving.**

# CHAPTER 8

# THE SCRIPT FOR YOUR NEW LIFE

You've heard the expression, "Today is the first day of the rest of your life." For most people that statement may be temporarily encouraging because it implies that just by realizing that fact we can let go of the past and start life anew. Unfortunately, without a fairly specific plan and some helpful techniques to replace negative programming with positive thoughts, images, and feelings we will continue moving inward on the spiral toward a more limited reality, financially and otherwise.

You may not have realized it yet, but by reading this far you have already begun mentally to rewrite the script for the rest of your life. You've learned how to deal with negativity, improve your self-image, and how to program yourself for the achievement of your written goals.

The remaining step is to actually write a script for the rest of your life as you, at this moment in time, choose it to be. As time goes by, you may decide to alter the script as you continue to learn and grow, but all you need to do is write a script based on your state of awareness and desires as of today. Keep in mind that your script is for *you*. No one else will read it unless you want them to.

Your script may be quite general and rather short such as:

My new life begins on this day: date _____

From this day forward I shall become more and more prosperous and I shall become financially independent by date _____. I will maintain this state of financial independence, and become additionally prosperous in keeping with my desires and goals throughout the rest of my life.

I will use my wealth wisely to help myself and others and to be a positive influence on this planet.

I will always keep in mind those things that I consider most important in life, such as family, friends, and my moral and spiritual values.

I will achieve my prosperity honestly, by providing good products and/or providing valuable services. I will use the techniques in this book to tap my creativity and use more of my potential every day.

The work that I do will be so rewarding and enjoyable it will be more like fun than work. On this day I will write my initial goals (at least one short-range, one medium-range and onc long-range goal) if I have not already done so.

I shall calm my mind and mentally program myself for the achievement of these goals at least twice a day. (At the beginning and end of each day.) I now carry my written goals with me and refer to them several times a day.

> I now clear or eject negatives and replace
> them with my favorite affirmations.

You may prefer to write a more complete and detailed script including your attainment of each goal; your specific income and/or net worth at various points in time; how you spend or invest your money; your home or homes; your other acquisitions; how you improve your health, relationships, golf game, and so on. You may also include how you develop your hidden talents, and how you help individuals or charities with your money.

Please take a few moments now to write your initial script on the blank pages following this chapter or on a pad of paper. Writing your script, even if it is very short, but positive, will speed up the process of attracting money and make the rest of your life more rewarding, enjoyable, and fulfilling.

# RESOURCES

## BOB'S TAPES (ALSO KNOWN AS THE LOVE TAPES®)

Alpha Break

Attracting More Love

Anger Control

Automatic Self-Discipline

Be Assertive

Being A Happy Parent

Better "Golden Years"

Blood Pressure

Business Success

Commitment and Persistence

Concentration

Conquering Fears

Coping with Death

Coping with Difficult and
   Negative People

Deep Relaxation

Decision Making

Developing Enthusiasm

Developing Creativity

Developing ESP

Discovering and Developing
   Your Talents

Dream Power

Drug and Alcohol Control

Effective Speaking

Effective Studying

Energy

Exercise Motivation

Freedom from Codependency

Getting a Good Job

Goal Achievement

Guilt Free

Health

How to Attract Money

How to Be Happy

Hot to Be Positive

Immunity and Longevity
Improve Your Luck
Improving Relationships
Inner Game of Selling
The Joy of Loving
The Joy of Sobriety
Learning Power
Letting Go of the Past
Loving Your Body
Managing Stress
Memory Power (Super Strength)
Morning and Evening
   Programming
Motivation
Overcoming Procrastination
Overcoming Worry
Pain Relief
Peace of Mind
Peak Performance in Sports
Personal Magnetism
Productivity and Organization

Restful, Revitalizing Sleep
Self-Confidence
Self-Image for Children
Self-Image
Sense of Humor
Slim Image II
Spiritual Healing
Stay Slim
Staying Young
Stop Smoking (Super Strength)
Successful Teens
Successful Marriage
Super Mind
Super Strength Self-Esteem
Super Strength Weight Loss
Surviving Separation
Taking Charge of Your Life
Up from Depression
Visualization Power
Winning

Although Effective Learning Systems, Inc., publishes no tapes that are strictly subliminal, the above titles are available with audible version on side A and the same words on side B recorded at a lower volume than the masking sound of beautiful music or ocean waves (your choice) so as to produce a subliminal effect.

The Regular (totally audible) tapes are $10.98 each (buy five and select five more free).

The Subliminal (audible on one side and subliminal on the other side) tapes are $12.98 each (buy five and select five more free).

Minnesota residents add 6.5% sales tax.
Shipping and handling—$3.00.
Send check or money order to:

Effective Learning Systems, Inc.
Dept. HTAM
5221 Edina Industrial Boulevard
Edina, MN 55439

For faster service call (612) 893-1680 for Visa, Discover, and MasterCard holders.

If you are out of work and can't afford the *Getting a Good Job* tape, just say so and we'll send it to you free. (Please include cost of shipping and handling.)

A free catalog of my tapes and those of Bernie Siegel, M.D., O. Carl Simonton, M.D., C. Norman Shealy, M.D., and other members of Effective Learning Systems, Inc., board of advisors will be enclosed with your tapes.